The Pedagogy of Possibilities: Developmental Education, College-Level Studies, and Learning Communities

National Learning Communities Project
Monograph Series

Gillies Malnarich

with

Pam Dusenberry

Ben Sloan

Jan Swinton

Phyllis van Slyck

Washington Center
for Improving the Quality of
Undergraduate Education

NATIONAL LEARNING COMMUNITIES PROJECT

The Evergreen State College
2700 Evergreen Parkway NW
Olympia, WA 98505
(360) 867-6910
fax (360) 867-6662
http://learningcommons.evergreen.edu

AMERICAN ASSOCIATION
FOR HIGHER EDUCATION

One Dupont Circle, Suite 360
Washington, DC 20036-1110
(202) 293-6440
fax (202) 293-0073
www.aahe.org

About the National Learning Communities Project

The National Learning Communities Project, based at The Washington Center for Improving the Quality of Undergraduate Education at The Evergreen State College, strives to strengthen curricular learning community efforts on individual college and university campuses, as well as to foster more robust communities of learning community practice. This monograph series brings together learning community leaders from across the country to explore critical issues related to theory and practice in learning community development, implementation, and assessment. The National Learning Communities Project (2000-03) is funded in part by a grant from The Pew Charitable Trusts.

About the American Association for Higher Education

The American Association for Higher Education promotes the improvement of higher education through work in four fields of inquiry and action (assessing for learning, learning about learning, partners in learning, and organizing for learning). An individual membership association, AAHE advances members' learning through research, convenings, projects, and publications. Its emphasis on praxis, the intersection of theory and practice, is an effective means to serve the higher education community in a complex, interconnected world. For more information about AAHE and membership, please visit www.aahe.org.

Acknowledgments

Thanks to the contributors to this monograph and to both Barbara Cambridge at AAHE and Barbara Leigh Smith at the National Learning Communities Project for their careful reading and suggestions, and to Sharilyn Howell for her persistent encouragement. Special recognition to Dena Jaskar, Sandra Abrams, and Esmé Ryan for editorial assistance, and to Mary Geraci for graphic design.

Caveat about URLs

Every effort has been made to reference active sites using current URLs, but as anyone familiar with the Web can attest, what's there today might well be gone tomorrow. If you cannot find a particular site, we suggest you search on a project's name.

Recommended bibliographic listing

Malnarich, G., with others. 2003. *The Pedagogy of Possibilities: Developmental Education, College-Level Studies, and Learning Communities*. National Learning Communities Project Monograph Series. Olympia, WA: The Evergreen State College, Washington Center for Improving the Quality of Undergraduate Education, in cooperation with the American Association for Higher Education.

Ordering Information

The Evergreen State College Bookstore	American Association for Higher Education
2700 Evergreen Parkway NW	Publications Fulfillment
Olympia, WA 98505	PO Box 1932
(360) 867-6215	Merrifield, VA 22116-1932
fax (360) 867-6793	fax (301) 843-9692
	www.aahe.org/pubs

ISBN 1-56377-064-4

Foreword

How do you treat people with respect? How do you do a program that treats people with respect?

Myles Horton in conversation with Paulo Freire,
We Make the Road by Walking

Paulo Freire and Myles Horton met in December 1987 for an extended conversation on education and social change. At one point, they were asked to talk about their approach to literacy work—Freire, the Brazilian educator, on popular education in Recife, and Horton, the founder of the Highlander Folk School, on Highlander's Citizenship Schools. Horton begins by describing Highlander's work in the 1950s on racial justice in the South and the integrated workshops held at Highlander that brought people together to learn from each other's experience. At one workshop, Essau Jenkins, a community leader who was trying to teach people to read while busing them to and from factory, mill, and domestic jobs in the city, asked for Highlander's help to set up a literacy school so people could pass the voter registration exam, gain the vote, and exercise political power.

When Horton stays at Jenkins' home on Johns Island so he can meet people who would attend the school, he discovers that literacy classes have been held on the island since before the Civil War up to the time of his visit. People start but never stay for long. Horton wants to know why and concludes that literacy workers did not treat people with respect. The two simple questions he asks himself—How do you treat people with respect? How do you do a program that treats people with respect?—guide planning for what will become a model for all Citizenship Schools. Horton and Jenkins, along with Septima Clark, a schoolteacher from Charleston, North Carolina, who once taught on Johns Island, draw up a few basic principles: black people should teach black people; the teachers should not be trained teachers who tend to treat adults like children; and, class materials should be challenging and closely resemble the difficult reading needed to pass the voter registration exam. Bernice Robinson, the first "teacher" chosen for her leadership qualities, wants people to learn to read things that will be inspiring to keep them motivated while they also learn desired skills such as writing their names and filling out money orders. She selects *The Declaration of Human Rights* and the Highlander mission statement to illustrate the theme of democracy and citizenship. To avoid the stigma of being in a literacy class, Robinson turns the class into a community organization—a Citizenship School—where people make plans for what they will do as a community when they get the vote. As Horton later remarks, " . . . reading and writing wasn't the purpose. Being a citizen was the purpose" (Horton and Freire 1990, 83).

Four years after the first class met in January 1957, the Citizenship Schools had trained 400 volunteer teachers. More than 4,000 people who attended the schools had passed the Citizenship School's final exam—to go down to the courthouse and register to vote. Andrew Young came to Highlander to coordinate the grassroots program and, in the early 1960s, it became the official program of the Southern Christian Leadership Conference (SCLC), its further expansion and integration into the civil rights movement coordinated by Young and Clark. By the 1970s, the SCLC estimated that around 100,000 people had learned to read and write at the Citizenship Schools. Later Horton would meet a woman who told him about the schools she and others "invented for their community," as indeed they had.

I like to think our best work in developmental education begins from this place of deep respect for learners, their learning and agency, and that this is true of our learning community work as well. The approach Horton describes, similar to the practice in other open education movements, does not rank learning from the least to the most prestigious. People value one another's experience, expect to learn from everyone present, and develop a camaraderie that is a good foil against frustration. No mention is made of "deficits" or "skill deficiencies." Why would people stigmatize others in this way?

When a group of fellows[1] from Washington Center's National Learning Communities Project (NLCP) met to discuss a proposed monograph on learning communities and developmental education, the question of respect came to mind as the conversation took a surprising turn early on. Should we use words other than "developmental education"?

The reasoning behind the question covered well-trod territory. Colleagues worry that faculty they know, including those teaching in college-level learning communities, might balk at reading something with developmental education in the title. On many campuses, developmental education is a code for remedial education or re-teaching basic skills that high school graduates and some middle school students should already know, hence the view that students taking developmental courses are "not smart." Colleagues report that where budget cuts force a rethinking of which programs and services should continue, heated exchanges tap into historically-persistent debates about developmental education: whether funds should be "diverted" from college-level programs to teaching (and learning) considered inappropriate for higher education; whether the influx of underprepared students dilutes academic expectations and lowers standards; and whether students in developmental education even belong in postsecondary education. As the conversation ran its course, it became clear that the proposed monograph could not address every perception about developmental education, however mistaken.

For readers interested in pursuing the above issues, there are several useful starting places. In *No One to Waste* (2000), Robert McCabe presents a data-rich defense of developmental education. In fact, developmental education turns out to be higher education's most productive program. At a cost of 1 percent of all higher education spending and 4 percent of financial aid, one million students are served, and approximately half of these students successfully complete developmental classes. Those who continue their studies do as well in standard college classes as their better-prepared peers. One-sixth complete academic undergraduate and associate degrees and one-third complete vocational degrees and certificates. In *Defending Access: A Critique of Standards in Higher Education* (1999), Tom Fox examines fears about declining literacy standards in the historical context of the push for access. He argues that cultural and/or linguistic differences are more at issue, not student performance. Fox urges us to break with acontextual standards in favor of context-specific and even student-specific standards. And, in *Who Belongs in College: A Second Look* (1998),

Carlette Hardin classifies developmental students into seven groups to counter the view that students are mainly eighteen-year-olds who slept through high school and want a second chance to learn at taxpayers' expense. Most fit the profile of "poor choosers," people who made decisions between ages fourteen and eighteen that continue to restrict their education and employment possibilities. Hardin also notes that when she first wrote about who belongs in college in 1988, developmental education's role in higher education was very contentious. A decade later, she reports that thirty-one states are embroiled in debates about its value—today, a mere five years later, the situation is even more volatile.

The Washington Center for Improving the Quality of Undergraduate Education's commitment to developmental education is deep-rooted. Both learning communities and developmental education have been influenced by the educational philosophies of Alexander Meiklejohn and John Dewey, specifically their views on democracy, education for citizenship, and a pedagogy that promotes "critical intelligence" as well as a developmental perspective on learning (Shaw 2002; Smith and McCann 2001; Smith, et al. Forthcoming). Back in 1985 when the Center began, the founders embraced developmental education as an essential component of higher education. Early in the center's history, Barbara Leigh Smith and Jean MacGregor organized a seminar, "Improving the Teaching of Basic Skills," where Roberta Matthews of LaGuardia Community College in New York City introduced "learning clusters" to Washington state educators. The example of LaGuardia's New Student House, a learning community model described later in this monograph, sparked people's interest. One of Washington Center's first curriculum planning retreats, "Creating Learning Communities for the Developmental Level Student," gave faculty teams from different campuses the time to plan integrated curriculum for underprepared students.

A modest seed grant program begun in the late 1980s helped good ideas sprout into practice. Early editions of the center newsletter report on emerging learning communities within developmental education, and among developmental education, English as a Second Language, and college-level courses. Some of these pioneering Washington state programs are featured in this monograph, not only for their commitment over the long haul, a key lesson in sustaining and leading organizational change, but also for another distinguishing hallmark—meaningful, engaged student learning. Other institutions featured in the monograph's case studies, such as De Anza, Grossmont, and LaGuardia community colleges, have equally long and distinguished learning community histories.

Opportunities to continue conversations with NLCP fellows helped clarify what two distinct and sometimes overlapping communities of reform-minded educators—faculty and academic staff involved in learning communities and faculty and academic staff involved in developmental education—do *not* know about one another's work and need to if we are to foster collaboration that will benefit underprepared students. The monograph's themes and topics reflect these exchanges.

Conversations with busy monograph contributors Pam Dusenberry, Ben Sloan, Jan Swinton, and Phyllis van Slyck turned into wonderful opportunities to explore the what, why, and how of working with students new to academic culture. Their accounts of learning community programs for developmental students, and the experience of others—drawn from National Learning Communities Project consultants' site visit reports, from Jean MacGregor's summaries of telephone interviews with developmental educators throughout the country, and from Washington Center's work with campus teams especially at curriculum planning retreats—illustrate possibilities for practice.

Readers are also invited to visit the learning communities directory on the National Learning Communities Project website for more resources and to register their own campus learning communities so we can all learn from one another's good work (http://learningcommons.evergreen.edu).

Endnotes

1. The "fellows" of the National Learning Communities Project are faculty, professional staff, and administrators from universities and community colleges across the country that are knowledgeable about learning community work and other educational reform efforts; they serve as consultants to the project and resource faculty for residential summer institutes.

Introduction

The Pedagogy of Possibilities: Developmental Education, College-Level Studies, and Learning Communities

Coming here turned my life around. We went on a field trip to the university and I realized . . . I could go there. If you work hard, ask for help, support each other, then we'll all make it.

J., a student from Pasadena City College's
Teaching and Learning Communities Bridge Program

Rising college attendance, falling completion rates, and a national dialogue on what is and is not working in higher education—the findings summarized eloquently in *Greater Expectations: A New Vision for Learning as a Nation Goes to College* (AAC&U 2002)—leads to a question that informs this monograph on learning communities for people unprepared and new to college-level studies: what kind of learning environments will both support and challenge students so more of them can meet our "greater expectations" while realizing their own? Learning communities are one response.

The monograph's title, *The Pedagogy of Possibilities*, intentionally brings to the fore people's high hopes and big dreams. The promise of an open door is about possibilities. Yet, we also know that many people's lives put them "at risk" in higher education even before they attend a college class.

We will examine what being at risk in higher education means in detail later on, but J., the young man quoted above, would certainly qualify. His story is similar to many of his classmates who live in the poorest neighborhood in their community college district. The first from their families to graduate from high school and to attend college, they serve as role models for brothers and sisters. Their stories illustrate the immense pressure they are under to be successful. Yet the fact that these young adults did not do well at school in the past is a defining marker. The odds are against J. and his peers "making it" at college. But they are also part of the first cohort to complete Pasadena City College's .XL summer bridge learning community, a doorway into the first-year experience teaching and learning communities program (TLC) that has been designed to help Hispanic and other underprepared students move successfully from basic skills to transfer and vocational programs.[1]

During the half-day I spent in the company of these students as part of a National Learning Communities Project site visit, I became more hopeful about higher education's possibilities. If these bright young women and men, and other students like them, can thrive and excel in their studies at campuses where we teach and work, then all students might ultimately benefit. Keen to learn, excited about the projects they are working on, and deeply appreciative of classmates' and TLC.XL faculty and staff's support, these students offer unsolicited evidence that education can be transformative and empowering.

In today's knowledge-based economy, with few exceptions, everyone belongs in college. Yet, the faculty members who confide to the authors of *Honored But Invisible: An Inside Look At Teaching in Community Colleges* (Grubb 1999) that students struggling in the back of their classes are not "college material," voice a concern that is not new in higher education. Students in the first college preparatory program in reading, writing, and mathematics established at the University of Wisconsin in 1849 provoked similar objections

(Brier 1984), even though the country's system of public schools[2] did not extend beyond the primary grades (Maxwell 1979). By 1865, 88 percent of this university's 331 students were enrolled in preparatory classes and only forty-one attended regular classes (Brubacher and Rudy 1976). Although the university eventually abolished its college preparatory program following intense attacks, other higher education institutions established similar programs to bridge the "academic preparation gap" (Brier 1984), a signal that higher education was no longer the prerogative of the sons of the very wealthy.

Colleges and universities have been providing academic support services for students less prepared than their classmates for more than a century and a half. From the early 1900s to the present, around 30 percent of all students entering colleges and universities have been developmental students (Boylan and White 1987; Roueche and Roueche 1993; McCabe 2000). During this time, the percentage of campuses offering preparatory, remedial, or developmental programs has been relatively constant. At the turn of the twentieth century, 84 percent of all colleges and universities in the country offered college preparatory programs (Abraham 1987); in 1915, 80 percent of institutions did so (Brubacher and Rudy 1976). In the 1980s and 1990s a similar percentage of institutions had learning assistance services and developmental education programs. During this same period, the National Study of Developmental Education estimated that 70 percent of four-year institutions and more than 90 percent of two-year institutions offered developmental courses (Boylan et al. 1992). In 1996, according to the National Center for Education Statistics, 78 percent of colleges and universities ran developmental courses. Current figures follow this pattern.[3]

Yet the presence of developmental programs and services at open admission two- and four-year campuses does not mean that new and underprepared students are viewed as legitimate members of the higher education community, even where the democratization of education is part of a founding ethos. For instance, in the community college sector that prides itself on making it possible for the poor, the working-class, and ethnic and racial minorities to become educated, the title of a study, *The Contradictory College* (Dougherty 1994), reflects inconsistent practices from one institution to another and among various subcultures within an institution. The instructors Grubb and his colleagues interview in *Honored But Invisible*, who decide some students don't belong in college, believe it is part of their job to dissuade people who "lack ability" from continuing academic studies. Other instructors make an effort to reassure students, as does this instructor who teaches in professional and technical programs: "I will tell the students when they first come to class, 'I don't care what area we are in, if you take me out of my environment and put me in your area, I would be all thumbs until I caught on. It's not that I don't have the intelligence to do it.' It's the same way in the classroom" (1999, 173). This mixed response to underrepresented students in higher education is evident from research findings: some institutional and instructional practices reinforce societal inequality where students new to academic culture, especially working-class students, are sorted into career and vocational tracks that "cool out" their aspirations (Brint and Karabel 1989; Zwerling 1976; Rhoads and Valdez 1996);

other studies describe exemplary programs and practices designed to empower students who arrive "differently prepared"[4] to the academy (Shaw 1997). Learning communities are emerging as a way of addressing some of these contradictions (Fogarty, Dunlap et al. 2003).

Worthy institutional mission statements can translate into multiple, competing goals in practice: broaden access, encourage diversity, uphold academic standards, increase retention rates. Developmental education—charged with the responsibility of keeping the open door open by ensuring that admitted students eventually become "ready" for college-level work—is often a battleground for working through an institution's conflicting purposes and practices. As Hunter Boylan points out in *What Works* (2002), a summary of more than twenty-five years of research-based practice in developmental education, faculty complaints that students do not belong at college and advisors' recommendations that students should avoid taking non-credit developmental courses so they can get on with the regular curriculum are indicators that developmental education is not an institutional priority or, even more telling, an institutional responsibility.

More than thirty years ago, Edmund Gleazer's response to the perennial complaint about whether some entering students are college material blames neither faculty failings nor student shortcomings for the challenges higher education faces:

> We are not building a college with the student. The question we ought to ask is whether the college is . . . student material. It is the student we are building, and it is the function of the college to facilitate that process. We have him as he is rather than as we wish he were . . . Can we come up with the professional attitudes . . . (to tap) pools of human talent not yet touched? (1970)

Gleazer emphasizes the responsibility of *an entire campus* to work with the mix of abilities people bring to the academy, no one kind of learning superior to another.

Gleazer's insights influenced a reform movement led by Terry O'Banion and the League for Innovation in the Community College in the mid-1990s to transform educational institutions into genuine learning organizations where all practices, from the classroom to the boardroom, would be vetted through a simple but powerful heuristic: how does this practice or policy or pedagogical intervention support or enhance student learning? (O'Banion 1997).

Earlier reform movements based on learner- and learning-centered ideas and practices have also defined fields within higher education. For instance, the Student Development Movement in the 1970s called on entire institutions and not only counselors and student affairs professionals to become more student centered. Twenty years earlier, Carl Rogers, a prominent leader in the Humanist Education Movement, drew insights from his studies of adults in therapy and applied them to education. His client-centered theory of personality and behavior became the foundation for his conceptualization of student-centered learning and the conviction that we cannot "teach" other people directly but can only "facilitate" their learning (1951; 1969). Rogers also introduced the concept of significant learning which involves the whole person: "significant learning . . . is more than an accumulation of facts. It is learning that makes a difference—in the individual's behavior, in the course of action he chooses in the future, in his attitudes, and in his personality . . . (it) interpenetrates . . . his existence" (1969, 280). These ideas shaped core practices not only within adult education (Kidd 1973; Knowles 1970; Knowles, et al. 1998), but also within developmental education through practitioners' study of adult learning theory and practice (Casazza and Silverman 1996). This intellectual legacy explains why faculty educated in these fields as well as student affairs professionals often contribute a seasoned expertise to learner- and learning-centered campus initiatives, including learning community work.

But as Robert Barr and John Tagg (1995) point out, most institutions in higher education are not organized to make student learning a central preoccupation even if some claim this is their mission and access far outstrips attainment. In their widely read and cited *Change* article, "From Teaching to Learning: A New Paradigm for Undergraduate Education," they note that most of us work in places where the institution is geared up to provide instruction, offer classes, and fill classes—patterns they associate with an "instructional paradigm." In times of tight budgets, struggling students are perceived as a liability; they drop out and drag publicly scrutinized retention rates down. Why admit them in the first place?

John Tagg deepens our understanding of how institutions' organizational structures and cultures undermine the high hopes and great expectations that students have for themselves and that we have for them and for higher education. In *The Learning Paradigm College* (2003), he points out that the functional frameworks of college life and college work, the everyday ways of doing and thinking about things, become so familiar we hardly notice them anymore, even when they impose limits on our collective ability to pay attention to student learning. He writes:

> What the Learning Paradigm proposes is simply to take hold of the horse and lead it to its proper position in the front of the cart, to put purposes before processes . . . Where the Instruction Paradigm highlights formal processes, the Learning Paradigm emphasizes results or outcomes. Where the Instruction Paradigm creates atomistic structures, the Learning Paradigm creates holistic ones. Where the Instruction Paradigm attends to classes, the Learning Paradigm attends to students. In the Learning Paradigm the mission of colleges and universities is to produce student learning. This end is primary; the means are secondary and are to be judged by how well they achieve the end. At the core of the Learning Paradigm is a model of the teaching-learning process that focuses on the learner learning. (31)

Tagg offers many examples of learning-centered practices, a number drawn from learning community practice (258–279). He captures the good sense and energy of learning communities by reminding us that on every campus we find vibrant, purposeful communities of practice with intentional learning goals and a mix of learners from novices to experts. The first examples he names we think of as extracurricular activities: math clubs, jazz ensembles, debating societies, newspapers, literary journals, theater groups, and so on. Learning communities also form *within the curriculum* so learning will be as engaging, purposeful, and powerful as learning outside school, and will link learning "in here" to learning "out there."

For J. and his peers, an off-campus ropes course—with its demanding mix of physical and emotional challenges—becomes a metaphor for academic success because to "do ropes" you must risk trusting yourself and others. A student who gives an impromptu lecture under a viaduct on the meaning of graffiti enthralls everyone during an inner-city field trip designed to introduce TLC.XL summer bridge students to the work of cultural anthropologists. This event becomes a story faculty tell their colleagues to explain why they find teaching developmental students transforming and worthy academic work. The field trip to the UCLA campus that leads J. to recast his lifetime possibilities surfaces in other students' stories. The field trip is "proof" the college believes each student *will* graduate. Why else would they be taken there?

What appears to be a naïve interpretation of an institution's role in student success is backed by educational research[5]; it is a view shared by educational reformers who appreciate that learning environments which offer the greatest support and most challenge for developmental students are part of a broader campus-wide commitment to improving *all* students' learning. In this sense, *The Pedagogy of Possibilities* is about more than isolated classroom practice, however superb an instructor's scholarly teaching, learning and assessment may be. We are interested in sites within the academy where a team of educators, working together and supported by administrative and institutional practices, are able to develop a holistic, integrative approach to student learning and student development that persists during a person's entire undergraduate experience.

In this monograph, we are especially interested in those sites where a learning communities' approach would most benefit students unprepared and new to college work and college life. Two places seem especially critical: within development education programs where students' placement assessments indicate their skills in reading, writing, and mathematics do not meet college entry expectations; and at transition points from developmental education into college-level courses, where students can become frustrated, flounder, and, if disconnected from supportive student subcultures, often leave college (Tinto 1987).

This monograph is divided into three sections. The first section lays the groundwork for collaboration by introducing higher education faculty and staff new or unfamiliar with developmental education and/or those unfamiliar with learning community work to one another's practice. We hope to dispel two notions: that developmental education is like a version of high school classes and any insights about teaching and learning will have little application to college-level work; and that learning communities, with their emphasis on substantive learning, are too intellectually demanding for students who need to work on basic skills.

The beginning chapter in the first section discusses what it takes to be "prepared" for college. We examine research on students' fear of failure, the approach to learning they subsequently adopt, and the conceptions of learning and intelligence that undermine effective learning. The second chapter introduces the work of developmental educators, a developmental perspective on learning, and research-based best practices in developmental education. The third chapter continues this discussion by examining learning communities, an acknowledged "best practice" and means for creating challenging and supporting learning environments for developmental students. We review the essentials of learning community practice from the original rationale to various curricular restructuring models, the architecture within which connected, meaningful student learning flourishes. A concluding call for action invites developmental educators and learning community practitioners to work together to not only support access to higher education, even if students arrive underprepared for college, but also to ensure that *all* students on our campuses are successful in their studies.

The monograph's second section offers more in-depth accounts of learning communities. These cases illustrate approaches to curriculum, and sometimes assignments, designed for developmental students in learning communities—either within developmental education or between developmental education and college-level studies. A third section on additional resources follows.

Endnotes

1. For more information on Pasadena City College's Teaching and Learning Communities Program go to http://www.pasadena.edu/externalrelations/TLC.
2. The system of public schools referred to did not include black children in the South.
3. See http://nces.ed.gov/ and Education Commission of the States 2002.
4. This expression is one used by De Anza College. See Stoll, 1999.
5. The National Center on Postsecondary Teaching, Learning, and Assessment's Out-of-Class Experiences Project reports that for first-generation college students "validation" is critical: "Faculty and staff validate a student when they tell the student that college is the right place for him or her, that others with similar backgrounds and abilities have attended college, and that this student, too, can succeed at the institution." See Ratcliff and Associates, 1995.

Table of Contents

I

Section One

Chapter 1

Taking A Risk to Learn: What It Means to be "Prepared" for Higher Education

Learning from its very beginnings entails a process of courting failure and learning to play with it.

John Tagg,
The Learning Paradigm College

This chapter briefly introduces expectations for higher education's graduates since intended outcomes give us a good idea of what kind of learning is valued in the academy, presumably for all students. But to create challenging and supportive learning environments for entering developmental students, we need to know about their experiences of learning. What factors contribute to being underprepared? What limits learning possibilities? How might we move students to a place where they can become fully engaged, confident learners, prepared to do college level work?

Educators want students to value the multiple perspectives and abilities of people unlike themselves and are prepared to make this an explicit part of students' education.

Articulating higher education's expectations

The most current thinking about learning outcomes for undergraduate education can be found in *Greater Expectations* (2002). This document is the product of a three-year dialogue, convened by the Association of American Colleges and Universities (AAC&U), where leading educators, campus teams, and hundreds of educators from across the country constructed a collective vision regarding the purpose of education, higher standards for all students, and a more successful kind of education that would reach more people. The invigorated, practical liberal education[1] called for intentionally unites liberal arts and professional and technical programs. The students we aim to graduate will be "empowered through the mastery of intellectual and practical skills; informed by knowledge about the natural and social worlds and about forms of inquiry basic to these studies; responsible for their personal actions and civic values" (xi). The report goes on to detail the learning students will need for the twenty-first century (21-28).

Greater Expectations also celebrates the diversity of students as a critical source for enriched, transformative learning. Educators want students to value the multiple perspectives and abilities of people unlike themselves and are prepared to make this an explicit part of students' education. The report, rich in its complexity, is also frank about pressing issues higher education needs to address, among these the fact that many entering students are not ready for college.

Arriving "underprepared" for college

Subheadings in *Greater Expectations* signal external circumstances or "barriers to readiness" that reduce the chances of academic success for some students well before they attend their first class: continuing patterns of separation and discrimination; limited interpretations of learning; a one-size-fits-all approach to assessment and to learning; uneven preparation for independent, demanding college-level study; and misalignment of high school work with college level expectations (12-15). We examine three of these circumstances in detail: the first, "misaligned expectations," where even the most academically able high school graduate may not be prepared for college; second, "risk factors" that indicate who is less likely to complete college and why; and third, the "academic achievement gap" that speaks to enduring school inequities and their effect on children's prospects for college.

Misaligned expectations

Pre-collegiate preparation depends on the extent to which a state's elementary and secondary school systems equip young people for college-level learning. In many states misaligned education systems are residuals from a time when few high school students continued their education at a college (Callan 2001). Now 75 percent of high school graduates in the country go on to postsecondary studies. Yet only 67 percent of these students earn standard high school diplomas and only 42 percent graduate with college-entry skills (McCabe 2000).

In many states, high school graduation standards are at a lower level than college-entry skills. As Robert McCabe notes in *Underprepared Students*, his response to *Measuring Up 2000: The State-by-State Report Card for Higher Education*: "Even with aggressive school reforms in place in many states, every year over one million academically underprepared students enter higher education and are in need of developmental, or remedial, education services" (2). This number translates into a picture that may surprise some educators: in fall 1995, the National Center for Educational Statistics found that 41 percent of first-time students in all undergraduate institutions took at least one developmental course in reading, writing, or mathematics (NCES 1996). Using data from student transcripts, the *High School and Beyond* study estimates that 63 percent of community college students and 40 percent of students at four-year colleges take at least one developmental course (Bailey 2001). Hunter Boylan (1995) notes that more than two million students are enrolled in various developmental reading, writing, and mathematics courses during a given academic year. This number excludes students enrolled in other developmental courses or an estimated 700,000 students in educational opportunity programs that offer developmental courses or services (Boylan and Saxon 1998).

Far from being a new trend, these figures confirm persistent findings over three decades that alarmed educators in the 1970s and throughout the 1980s and 1990s. Between 1970 and 1979, the verbal SAT scores of college freshmen declined by 40 points and math SAT scores declined by 18 points (Roueche et al. 1984). In the 1980s, the majority of freshmen going to community colleges read below the eighth grade level, a decline in two grade levels from 1971 (Trow 1983). Another study revealed that one-half of high school seniors could not solve problems with fractions and decimals and more than 85 percent could not write and think analytically in English (NCES 1991). By 1990, a broader newspaper-reading public knew about the nationwide "basic skills crisis" and its implications for American society and the country's schools (Sprout 1990).

Risk factors

What does it mean for students to be "at risk" in higher education? A report from the Community College Survey of Student Engagement (CCSSE),

Pre-collegiate preparation depends on the extent to which a state's elementary and secondary school systems equip young people for college-level learning.

Engaging Community Colleges: A First Look (2002), identifies eight risk factors that indicate who is least likely to meet their educational goals in higher education. Six factors represent what many of us would regard as an account of an *ordinary life*: someone who works more than thirty hours a week, cares for children at home, is a single parent, attends school part-time, pays his or her own college costs, and thinks the expense of going to college is a "significant issue." Two other risk factors describe either a family's historic relationship to higher education, that is, being a first-generation college student, or an individual's experience of schooling, that is, being academically underprepared. The indicators for this last risk factor include not earning a high school diploma and/ or participating in or planning to participate in developmental education. Based on a survey CCSSE field tested in spring 2002, 66 percent of the approximately 33,500 students surveyed from forty-eight community and technical colleges are at moderate-risk indicated by two to four risk factors, while 9 percent are high-risk with five or more risk factors present in their lives.

Among risk factors, being academically underprepared is clearly a red flag. The more students need developmental education, the less likely they are to persist in their studies and graduate (Astin 1985). At-risk students typically begin their post-secondary studies having experienced negligible academic success in elementary and secondary schools; they also have weak self-concepts and inappropriate or poorly defined goals (Cross 1971, 1976; Maxwell 1979).

The League for Innovation in the Community College in *Serving Underprepared Students* (1990) reports that a disproportionate percentage of at-risk students are minorities from urban areas. The category of at-risk students also includes students with limited proficiency in English, immigrants, high school graduates, returning adults, high school leavers, and illiterate adults.

In *Between A Rock and a Hard Place* (1993), the Roueches do not mince words regarding higher education's responsibility to the at-risk student:

> All schools, colleges, and universities across the nation are failing at unconscionable levels to effectively meet the needs of the students that they enroll . . . we are being confronted with increasing numbers of students that we simply are not teaching effectively. The problem will not go away . . . (vii)

The Roueches note that 75 percent of high school seniors may theoretically qualify for college, but "they are clearly not equipped to do regular college work" (4). They estimate that as many as one-third to one-half of all incoming students to higher education meet the standard definition of at-risk. Compared to four-year colleges and universities, the student population at community colleges is three to four times more likely to reflect risk factors.

Academic achievement gap

As McCabe points out in *No One to Waste* (2000), "poverty has the highest correlation with educational underpreparation at every level, from preschool to graduate school" (12). His chapter on "Why America Depends on Community

College Remedial Education" is a disturbing account of successive governments' failed promises and the effects on the country's poorest citizens, especially the one in five children who grow up with none of the economic and educational advantages of their better-off peers. Test results by race/ethnicity in letter-writing and checkbook-balancing reveal the underbelly of the basic skills crisis. Only 60 percent of young Hispanics and 40 percent of young African Americans pass literacy and numeracy tests compared to 80 percent of white, non-Hispanic young people, the disparity in results attributed to the high correlation among poverty, undereducation, and minority status (Roueche and Roueche 1993). McCabe (2000) reports that at college, 60 percent of developmental education students are white non-Hispanic, 23 percent are African American, and 12 percent are Hispanic. Each minority group is over represented, a pattern already evident in public school.

Impoverished neighborhoods, poorly funded schools, and curriculum stripped of its academic content lead to what Jonathan Kozol (1991) calls "savage inequalities" and Robert Moses (2001) refers to as a sharecropper's education for children of color and the poor. Higher levels of poverty among Hispanic American and African American households are reflected in data on academic performance. By the ninth grade, only 84 percent of children who begin school are still enrolled. Of these remaining young people, another 16 percent will drop out before graduation. Within this group, 25 percent of Hispanic American teenagers and 13 percent of African American teenagers will leave school, compared to about 8 percent of white non-Hispanic teens (McCabe 2000).

The disparities among children are well documented by the eighth grade. For instance, in Minnesota, the top-performing state in mathematics proficiency, 35 percent of eighth graders score at or above proficiency levels on national assessments of math compared to only 7 percent in Louisiana and Mississippi. Throughout the country, 31 percent of all eighth graders score at or above proficiency levels while only 9 percent of low-income eighth graders achieve similar scores. These results are not unique to mathematics (see *Measuring Up 2000*), although the educational consequences of innumeracy are particularly devastating. In *Radical Equations: Civil Rights from Mississippi to the Algebra Project* (2001), Moses spells out the broader consequences for a people and a country:

> In today's world, economic access and full citizenship depend crucially on math and science literacy. I believe that the absence of math literacy in urban and rural communities throughout this country is an issue as urgent as the lack of registered Black voters was in Mississippi in 1961 . . . math literacy—and algebra in particular—is the key to the future of disenfranchised communities. (5)

Moses calls this cutting off of economic access the civil rights issue of our times. For the last thirty years, this former civil rights leader and mathematician has harnessed his talents to teaching high school students algebra and to organizing the Algebra Project,[2] a grass roots movement for the transformation of mathematics education. Without a decisive intervention in children's schooling by the eighth grade, similar to the work done by the Algebra Project, young African Americans, Hispanics, and poor whites will be sidelined from the mainstream of economic and social life before they reach high school. For the very small percentage of students from impoverished neighborhoods who make it to higher education, developmental programs are not a second chance but instead represent a first opportunity to learn what has been missing from their public education. Simply surviving school to make it to college (including returning to school after a long absence) turns out to be an incredible achievement for many developmental and at-risk students. Staying in college beyond the first year also represents a victory: over half of all students enrolled in higher education drop out in the first year, 68 percent of students at two-year institutions compared to 53 percent at four-year institutions (Tinto et al.1994).

If we track what happens to people whose life circumstances make attending and staying in college a heroic expedition, we come face-to-face with a sobering snapshot, captured in a single table that compares college graduates, aged twenty-four, from high-income families with those from low-income families: 7 percent of poor youth obtain a bachelor's degree compared to 48 percent of their wealthier peers (Education Trust 1998). These figures speak to an estrangement between the academy's expectations for its graduating students—our *Greater Expectations*—and higher education's collective inability to deliver on the egalitarian and democratic promise of access and educational opportunity for all.

Gauging the impact of educational quality on degree completion

Clifford Adelman's landmark study, *Answers in the Tool Box: Academic Intensity, Attendance Patterns, and Bachelor's Degree Attainment* (1999), offers a comprehensive portrait of which factors contribute most to degree completion. He uses high school and college transcripts, test scores, and surveys to follow the school histories of a national cohort beginning in 1980 when students are in the tenth grade to 1993 when they are around thirty years of age.

Based on findings from this study, Adelman questions the significance of variables long associated with college completion such as the level of parents' education or persistence from first to second year unless they are connected to students' academic standing: how significant is being on a college preparatory track if few Carnegie units are earned in core academic subjects? Is part-time enrollment as telling a variable as the "DWI" index, the number of drops/ withdrawals/incompletes compared to the total number of courses a student attempts? Variables that Adelman's study indicate are critical to college completion include three findings which reveal the vital connection between being prepared for higher education and misaligned expectations, risk factors, and the academic achievement gap. The first finding is that "academic intensity and quality of secondary school curriculum" has the greatest impact on degree completion, including for African American and Latino students, compared to other pre-college academic indicators such as test scores and class rank/ academic GPA (84-86). In fact, academic resources (the composite of high

Simply surviving school to make it to college (including returning to school after a long absence) turns out to be an incredible achievement for many developmental and at-risk students.

school curriculum, test scores, and class rank) is a far more telling indicator of academic success than socioeconomic status (24-25). A second and related finding indicates that the higher the level of mathematics studied the greater the likelihood of degree completion (16-18). For instance, successfully completing a course beyond Algebra 2 such as trigonometry or pre-calculus more than doubles the odds that a student will complete a bachelor's degree. The third finding is that the type and amount of remediation students require is tied to degree completion: 39 percent of four-year college students that placed in remedial reading courses completed degrees compared with 60 percent who took one or two other types of remedial courses, and 69 percent who did not require remediation (79).

The critical importance of the intensity and quality of high school curriculum to degree completion led Adelman to conclude that "opportunity-to-learn is our most important objective." He notes that students need to take advantage of these opportunities; they need to be supported by school, peer, and family environments; and these opportunities-to-learn need to occur inside and outside school. Adelman's study also suggests that *curriculum quality* needs to be emphasized in developmental education programs—the bridge between students' often inadequate and poor educational experience in high school and demanding college-level courses.

The enormous challenges facing higher education are clear if we return to the students who took the ropes course. Since 2000, the TLC Program at Pasadena City College has staked out an ambitious agenda—to reverse a troubling trend on the third largest single campus in the country, where 40 percent of nearly 26,000 students failed in 1999, fewer than 4 percent transferred to the California university system, and less than 6 percent received certificates or degrees.[3] Minorities make up 80 percent of the student body (37 percent self-identified as Latinos, 32 percent as Asian Pacific Americans, 4 percent as Filipino, 7 percent as African American, 20 percent as white, and less than 1 percent as American Indian). Many students are first-generation; two-thirds go to school part-time; 66 percent of their teachers are adjunct faculty. Student services are available in thirteen languages—Arabic, Armenian, Cantonese, Mandarin, Dutch, French, Italian, Japanese, Korean, Russian, Spanish, Tagalog, and Vietnamese. The college continues to affirm its mission as an open door, comprehensive institution for transfer, vocational, and developmental education and for adult basic education students who are over eighteen years of age, with or without high school graduation, who can profit from the instruction offered.

But, when students move on from the Title V-funded project, will the college continue to give the young students I met the ongoing support they already know they will need to be successful? Will the college be able to scale-up this learning community pilot to meet other entering students' needs? Would any of our campuses, faced with similar challenges?

Differentiating between degrees of underpreparedness

In 1979, a decade after an open door policy became the norm in higher education, Martha Maxwell—founder of learning centers and reading and study skills programs at several universities, and leader of an annual institute at Berkeley for directors and staff of college learning centers throughout the country—addressed the question of "who are the underprepared students?" She did so from the perspective of an insider, charged with implementing higher education's promises to its least prepared students. At the time, Maxwell was very familiar with problems students had in adapting to the academic demands of college and with the learning support services colleges provided to help them. She had worked as a counselor, academic advisor, reading/learning disabilities specialist, and teacher of special programs for low achieving college students and adults for many years. Given her experience, Maxwell did not settle for a simple definition of academic underpreparedness.

In *Improving Student Learning Skills* (1979), she notes that students can be misprepared for college-level studies through poor choices made at some point in their lives where they (or others) select a program that does not prepare them for college-level work. Courses taken in high school may not reflect college-level expectations or the two educational systems may not be aligned, graduating expectations a poor fit with incoming expectations. Other students are simply underprepared; they leave high school before graduating. For some adult learners with either physical or learning disabilities, college may be the first opportunity to fill in missing educational pieces. Some adult learners, away from school for extended periods of time, forget what they once knew. Most students will struggle with the expectation that they are responsible for their own learning. Maxwell expects that the majority will also be anxious and fearful of failure when faced with escalating academic difficulties.

Underpreparedness is relative, Maxwell argues. Compared to capable peers, underprepared students are "those whose skills, knowledge, and academic ability are significantly below those of the 'typical' student in the college or curriculum in which they are enrolled" (3). By this definition, whether someone is underprepared for college depends on the particular institution—its entrance standards, the expectations of its faculty, and the characteristics of its average students—and the students' own degree of preparedness. In other words, college readiness and the possibilities for success are highly contextualized and institutionally based. Entering freshmen can be underprepared not only in relation to entrance standards, but also in relation to particular departments' prerequisites or expectations, either explicit or implicit. Instructors' expectations about college level work differ too even if they teach courses with an identical title and number. Assignments given to incoming students, from writing-intensive research reports to problem-based projects to multiple-choice exams, are among the most significant indicators of differences.

Maxwell offers this caution: "The strongly motivated, high-achieving student will succeed despite poor teaching and inappropriate materials, but the underprepared student will not"(x). In her experience, "the further students fall below the college's norm, the more likely they are to have serious academic difficulties, and the harder it is to help them" (3-4). She advocates using various placement assessments to determine degrees of underpreparedness and the best combination of academic support services for each student. Maxwell's practical guide on the planning and assessment of student-centered developmental programs and learning assistance centers continues to be influential (see revised edition of *Improving Student Learning Skills* 1997).

Courses taken in high school may not reflect college-level expectations or the two educational systems may not be aligned, graduating expectations a poor fit with incoming expectations.

. . . turns on its head the question of whether students are prepared for higher education and asks whether higher education can change sufficiently to be prepared for its "New Students."

Although Maxwell does not think that one developmental program or service can meet the diverse needs of all misprepared or underprepared students, she outlines essential features of an effective, integrated approach to working with developmental students: (1) student services and academic departments should coordinate efforts; (2) students, including those with learning disabilities, should be treated as adults and full participants in planning academic support services; and, (3) teachers should use appropriate, college-related materials along with methods designed to help students with learning problems learn. A variety of learning community models have been developed that build on these important insights, which will be discussed in chapter three.

Understanding the challenges posed by "New Students"

In *Beyond the Open Door* (1971), K. Patricia Cross turns on its head the question of whether students are prepared for higher education and asks whether higher education can change sufficiently to be prepared for its "New Students." Although her "new educational program for New Students" never made it onto the educational reform agenda, it is still worth looking at because it focuses on what continues to be most problematic about educational programs for underprepared students—the inattention paid to curriculum and teaching quality in relation to many non-traditional students' distinctive approaches to learning.

In *Honored But Invisible* (1999), for instance, Grubb and his colleagues are critical of a "student support" pedagogical approach that assumes if students are given sufficient encouragement they will develop into autonomous, empowered learners who can learn anything: "This approach describes a role for instructors (or student service personnel like counselors) in their personal relations with students. However, it is silent about every other element of teaching: how to present academic or occupational content, appropriate goals for learning, what assessment should be devised, the responsibilities of students. In our interpretation 'student support' in its extreme form is really an evasion of teaching responsibility rather than a distinctive approach" (36). They review award-winning developmental programs and conclude that most programs for low-achieving students provided "student services such as tutoring, mentoring, and counseling but left the basic teaching of remedial/developmental courses alone. These programs implicitly assumed that student support is sufficient for student success, even if core teaching is poor" (36). Cross addresses these issues in *Beyond the Open Door* by analyzing non-traditional students' prior experiences of learning in relation to the *educational programs* offered by colleges.

Like Gleazer and Tagg, Cross is interested in institutional and system-wide practices. Her critique, though, focuses on higher education's rigid adherence to an educational model designed only for traditional students, despite evidence thirty years ago (and now) that droves of non-traditional students enter and then leave postsecondary education within their first year. Even so, Cross did not emphasize retention:

Major energies have been directed toward getting New Students into college and keeping them there. Open admissions, special recruitment of disadvantaged students, and financial-aid programs are practices in widespread use throughout the country to attract New Students to college . . . Since getting New Students into—and preferably through—college has been the almost single-minded goal, virtually all evaluation of our achievements has been concerned with quoting statistics on increased rates of access and retention. Only recently have a few scattered voices questioned whether recruitment and retention are really the goals. I think they are not. The goal of educators is to educate. We have, however, sold out to the false god of certification, and in our eagerness to get degrees into the hands of New Students we are afraid to ask ourselves whether we are *educating* them. (1971, 163)

Cross argues for "a new education for New Students" (155-74). She insists that she does not think that new students are simply "less skillful" than others; instead, they approach learning in a radically different way. This point has profound implications for developing effective curriculum for developmental students; Cross advises developmental educators to "provide a new perception of the learning process" (31).

Cross based her analysis of the critical challenge facing higher education—to transform the what and how of learning to accommodate *all* students' learning needs—on data from national studies. She discovered that students coming to the academy in the late 1960s and 1970s differed from their traditional predecessors in one critical way: throughout their schooling, in traditional tests of academic achievement based on traditional curricula, they consistently ranked in the bottom third of their class. Low test scores, more than any other available measure including race, gender, and socioeconomic status, separated these New Students from others. Cross anticipated that a continuing emphasis on access programs would bring increasing numbers of what she refers to as "low-ability students" into higher education.

In 1971, most of these New Students—"swept into college by the rising educational aspirations of the citizenry"—were white, although a substantial number were from minority ethnic groups (15). Their fathers worked at blue-collar jobs and most were first-generation students who did not know what to expect from college. Most came from educationally and financially impoverished backgrounds and suffered the effects of low family education levels, discrimination, and poverty. Her analysis also indicated that more than a quarter of these students who did not do well in traditional education came from families where fathers did have college educations.

Fear of failure

Cross uses a striking metaphor to help educators understand what the influx of new students will mean for higher education (Cross 1971, 22). She compares traditional students, who throughout their schooling place in the top third of their class, to strong swimmers who move through the water with relative ease, getting better and increasingly confident with practice. New students are like weak swimmers. Thrown into downstream currents above a waterfall, fearful of drowning, they try to keep from going over. Strong swimmers swim to calm

She insists that she does not think that new students are simply "less skillful" than others; instead, they approach learning in a radically different way.

waters and focus on how fast they are swimming. As Cross notes, these achievement-oriented learners approach learning tasks of intermediate ability with a fifty-fifty chance of being successful: "This approach describes what we ordinarily think of as efficient learning, moving to progressively higher levels of accomplishment in small increments" (22). Weak swimmers, the students at the bottom third of the class academically, *are* learning at school too, but most are learning how to avoid failure: "For the fear-threatened individual, the task of intermediate difficulty is most likely to be avoided in favor of non-threatening tasks of assured success or of no probability of accomplishment . . . To do something you already know how to do is not learning. Neither is trying something that you cannot possibly do" (168-169).

The students who graduate in the bottom one-third of their class, schooled in methods to avoid failure, also avoid learning. The challenge is to spark students' curiosity so they will risk learning something a bit beyond what they already know and can do, and will gradually move from accomplishment to accomplishment. Cross points out that "successful remediation programs would need to devote considerable attention to a total reorientation of the students' approach to learning situations" (26). New students, Cross contends, approach learning differently than their more successful peers.

> To change a failure-threatened student into an achievement-oriented learner involves a fundamental change in attitude. It means that the learner must become eager to test himself instead of becoming motivated to find ways of avoiding the test of personal competency. It means that the student must become curious about himself and what he can do instead of being afraid to find out . . . The goal of reorienting the New Student to learning is to change attitudes, but the student must also be given ample practice in learning. (169-170)

Educational programs for "New Students"
But what kind of education should we offer "New Students"? Cross scrutinizes the programs offered to these students and reaches this conclusion.

> We are in the grip of a 'deficiency' conception of New Students. From nursery school to college, we give more attention to correcting the weaknesses of New Students than to developing their strengths . . . By the time students reach 17 and 18 years of age, their patterns of learning and behaving are much more firmly established than those of four- and five-year-olds, and compensatory programs in community colleges are not going to make many New Students over into traditional students. Furthermore, we have not been able to demonstrate that performance in the traditional discipline-bound curriculum is related to adult success. Why, then, do we try so hard to reach a goal that is probably both unattainable and undesirable? (Cross 1971 57-58)

The deficiency model, as Grubb and his colleagues point out in their recent analysis of instructors' approaches to pedagogy—based on interviews with people

"For the fear-threatened individual, the task of intermediate difficulty is most likely to be avoided in favor of non-threatening tasks of assured success or of no probability of accomplishment . . . To do something you already know how to do is not learning. Neither is trying something that you cannot possibly do"

from 32 community colleges across the country and 257 classroom visits and observations—is far more pervasive than educators imagine.

> The conventional approach to teaching often embodies several assumptions about intelligence: that it is relatively fixed rather than malleable, and that it is single-dimensioned rather than multiple-dimensioned. The notions of relatively fixed intelligence or ability leads to an emphasis on screening mechanisms and prerequisites, with the aim of tracking students based on their perceived abilities. This also fits with the view that students who score poorly on diagnostic tests are deficient, lacking the skills and knowledge that would enable them to score at the right level. The language of deficiency is quite common in conventional instruction, particularly in remedial and developmental education . . . The assessment of deficiency then slides over into assumptions that students are to blame for their deficiencies—that they are stupid, or that they come from intellectually impoverished families and communities—and this reasoning is frequently applied to the "disadvantaged" students who have not done well in school. (Grubb and associates 1999, 31)

Cross introduces her proposal for a new education for New Students by rephrasing a question John Gardner posed in 1961, "can we be equal and excellent too?" and asks, "can we be *different* and excellent too?" (Cross 1971, 160). She bases her proposal on a three-part functional analysis of the work world: people are needed to work with people, to work with things, and to work with ideas. She imagines that students would develop excellence not in fragmented, course-based curriculum but in one of three spheres with the expectation that they would develop at least minimal competence in the other two. She writes, "The potentially excellent mechanic may need tutoring in English, and the future excellent college professor may need tutoring in the fundamentals of machine repair. Both are handicapped in the modern world without minimum competence in the other's sphere of excellence" (165). Cross uses the example of an academically successful youth from the upper-middle class to make her case for how a new vision for education would be less skewered in favor of traditional students:

> . . . [I]t is intriguing to think about the new perceptions that might be gained as he copes with the intricacies of machine repair . . . discovers that he lacks the vocabulary to know one machine part from another . . . find(s) that while he is trying to use *his* developed skill in reading the repair manual, the instructor is "moving too fast" in a field that does not depend on verbalization. To add to his difficulties, he finds that his parents are totally unable to help him because that kind of learning is not in their background and the materials for learning are not easily available in the home. In other words, a student who has always been successful in school finds himself "educationally disadvantaged." (166)

The conventional approach to teaching often embodies several assumptions about intelligence: that it is relatively fixed rather than malleable, and that it is single-dimensioned rather than multiple-dimensioned.

Addressing students' approaches to learning

As Cross suggests, faculty can entice fear-of-failure students to risk learning if the environment is supportive and the educational project is interesting enough so natural curiosity takes over. But findings from a series of adult education studies first undertaken in Sweden, the United Kingdom, and Australia (Marton, Hounsell, and Entwistle 1984; Ramsden 1988), reveal a further dimension to how students' approaches to learning limit possibilities for learning even if curriculum is engaging.

In many of these studies, students read articles, often on controversial public issues, and summarized their understanding. Some students grasped the underlying structure of what they read and the deeper, intended meaning of the writer, while other students recalled scattered details and disjointed points that mixed the author's ideas with their opinions. These findings, described by researchers as processing that occurs on a "deep level" as compared to processing that skips along the "surface" of the text, led researchers to experiment with how teaching and assessment influence the quality of student learning. After a series of studies, researchers discovered that what students think they are supposed to learn—that is, their understanding of the purpose of learning—influences their approach to learning. For instance, if students have a Trivial Pursuits conception of knowledge (Dahlgren 1984), where *how much* someone knows is a measure of intelligence, then they will read to collect information to recall later—names, dates, numbers, and discrete facts—since real experts answer increasingly detailed questions that no one else can. If they think learning is about *what* is known and changes in thinking, then they will be on the lookout for a writer's perspective and key ideas. This research suggests that to influence students' approaches to learning, including developmental students, we would need to address students' conceptions of learning directly, a critical first step before working with students on basic skill development (Malnarich 1994).

Insights from ongoing studies allowed researchers to refine early notions of deep and surface processing levels to the now well-known conceptual distinction between *deep and surface approaches to learning* (Entwistle 2000). In a surface approach "the student intends merely to cope with course requirements in a minimalist fashion" and "learns by passively reproducing" (10): learning is equated with memorizing; understanding is limited to "question spotting" for tests; and course content is reduced to unrelated, discrete bits of knowledge. In a deep approach "the student intends to understand ideas for himself or herself" and "learns by actively transforming" (10): new ideas are related to previous knowledge and experience; underlying principles and patterns are sought out; evidence is examined in relation to conclusions; and, the logic of an argument is critically appraised.

Approaches to learning and developing basic skills

Experiments done by Ference Marton and Roger Säljö (1984) indicate that the questions instructors typically ask students about reading passages, even those designed to direct students' attention to deeper understanding, encourage "technification" (50). As Lennart Svensson (1984) points out, skills are techniques that have a functional relationship to approaches to learning.

After a series of studies, researchers discovered that what students think they are supposed to learn—that is, their understanding of the purpose of learning—influences their approach to learning.

A study undertaken at the University of Melbourne in Australia (Ramsden et al. 1986) underscores how skill development alone does not challenge the complex relationships between what students think learning is, faculty expectations, how students interpret faculty expectations given their conceptions of learning, and what they actually learn. In the study, faculty and staff worked with students in learning skill groups. They evaluated students' approaches to learning before and after their experience in these groups. The results are what Marton and Säljö, and then Svensson observed—as I have in work with developmental students. Instructional intervention led to even greater incidences of surface approaches to learning: "students actively and critically extract from skills programmes what is useful to them; 'what is useful' is a function of their perceptions of the requirements of assessment and teaching" (1986, 161-62), or their conceptions of learning.

... "students actively and critically extract from skills programmes what is useful to them; 'what is useful' is a function of their perceptions of the requirements of assessment and teaching" ...

Approaches to learning and conceptions of intelligence

John Tagg connects findings from research on deep and surface learning with research on self-theories and academic motivation to provide us with a powerful argument for why we need to explicitly address students' conceptions of learning and conceptions of intelligence soon after they arrive at college (2003, 48-86). In an academic context, students tend to adopt distinct achievement goals, ones that are either performance-oriented or learning-oriented. Tagg cites the work of Carol Dweck to illustrate the difference: performance goals are "about winning positive judgments of your competence and avoiding negative ones"; learning goals are about increasing competence and deepening understanding (Dweck 2000, 48-49).

Dweck's research further suggests that students choose one set of goals over another set based on their conceptions of intelligence. Students who adopt an entity theory where intelligence and/or ability is understood to be a fixed and immutable quantity—*you are either smart or stupid, you get it or you don't*—are more likely to be performance oriented. Students who adopt an incremental theory where intelligence and/or ability is understood to be changeable and contingent—*it takes time to learn, hard work pays off*—are more likely to be learning-oriented.

Dweck concludes that self-theories more than self-confidence influence students' approaches to learning. Entity-believing, performance-oriented students expect quick results. To experience frustration when learning indicates a lack of ability. Why try? Yet, as Tagg observes:

> None of us would be walking or talking—and certainly not reading, writing, and calculating—had we not embarked at an early age on the systematic project of doing things that were definitely impossible for us and repeatedly failing at them for an extended period of time. Those of us who have observed young children learning to walk or talk have noticed that toddlers are so called because they do not fear falling down and often seem to positively enjoy it. Toddlers are all incremental theorists and embrace learning goals with gusto. (2003, 54)

To alter people's life circumstances before they come to college is a tall order. Still, we can do our collective best to support students' aspirations once they arrive in higher education.

Students who are entity theorists, on the other hand, combine a set of beliefs that undermine our best efforts to promote self-directed, empowered learning.

The CCSSE report quoted earlier notes that "high-risk students appear to be exerting more effort to succeed . . . because they are overcoming significant challenges to attend college" (2002, 9). We learn that many at-risk students come prepared to class, ask questions, participate in discussions, do two or more drafts of a paper or assignment before handing it in, find exams "extremely or quite difficult," and devote as much time to preparing for class and studying as they do at work (79 per cent of the high-risk group work more than thirty hours per week compared to 6 percent of the low-risk group). They use learning assistance services and are more likely to give high ratings to the importance of tutoring, skill labs, financial aid advising, and career counseling. The more risk factors students face, the more likely they are "to participate in study-skills classes, a college orientation and success course, and organized learning communities" (9). These determined students are found throughout the academy. They tend to be the ones who seek constant and substantive feedback on their work, stick to their studies despite frustration, and appreciate that advances in learning depend on their efforts.

To alter people's life circumstances before they come to college is a tall order. Still, we can do our collective best to support students' aspirations once they arrive in higher education. Practices associated with an "instruction paradigm"—such as an atomistic orientation to knowledge, a surface approach to learning, and an entity theory of intelligence (Tagg 2003)—represent substantial yet unnamed risk factors when combined with underprepared students' often dismal school histories, ineffective approaches to learning, and limiting self-theories. What is the value in replicating educational practices that hamper students' ability to learn semester after semester, quarter after quarter?

Endnotes

1. The Greater Expectations National Panel Report defines liberal education as "a philosophy of education that empowers individuals, liberates the mind from ignorance, and cultivates social responsibility" (2002, 25).
2. For information on the Algebra Project go to http://www.algebra.org/index.html.
3. As Adelman points out in his study, 60 percent of undergraduates attend more than one institution: "It is not wise to blame a college for superficially low graduation rates for the behavior of students who swirl through the system."

Chapter 2

Adopting a Developmental Perspective in the Academy: Practices that Support and Enhance Student Learning

All our students struggle at some point during the undergraduate curriculum, and their learning is the collective responsibility of the entire institution, not just the specialized staff.

Cromwell et al. *Thriving in Academe*

This chapter examines the history of working with underprepared students in higher education in relation to contemporary challenges identified in *Greater Expectations* (AACU 2002). As this report points out: "At the heart of the Greater Expectations vision is the belief that everyone is entitled to an education of quality" (11). The report, which does not explicitly discuss developmental education, calls for a shift in national priorities away from access alone to two interconnected goals: "access to college learning of *high quality* for every student" and "appropriate preparation for all to *succeed* at this demanding level" (11). What practices support and enhance learning within the classroom and across an entire campus?

Evolving practice of developmental education

An account of the historical and continuing role played by developmental education in higher education shows how indispensable the field has been to the democratization of higher education and how reluctant higher education has been to acknowledge its contributions (McCabe and Day 1998). Brier offers this summary: "bridging the academic preparation gap has been a constant in the history of American higher education . . . and the controversy surrounding it is an American educational tradition" (Brier 1984, 2). The Roueches, who have written extensively on developmental education, reach this conclusion: "historically, programs for at-risk students were low status, low priority, and isolated on a college's organizational chart" (Roueche and Roueche 1993, 71). Yet for people who believe democracy requires an educated citizenry where access to education is extended to everyone, the rationale for why developmental education belongs in higher education is found in the stories and numbers of people who arrive unprepared, persist in their studies, and graduate.

The history of developmental education in higher education also allows us to appreciate the origins and intended purposes of various curricular and pedagogical practices still in use and, given our times and aims, to evaluate whether they meet the *Greater Expectation* goal of appropriate preparation for college learning.

Overview of developmental education within higher education

Access to mainstream higher education has depended on a mix of factors from enabling federal legislation backed by funding incentives[1] to political pressure created by citizens' organizing efforts. At critical junctures in the push for greater access, various versions of "developmental education"[2] became the only means for students, already admitted with tuition paid, to learn how to do college-level work. One of these first junctures occurred in 1862, when the

An account of the historical and continuing role played by developmental education in higher education shows how indispensable the field has been to the democratization of higher education and how reluctant higher education has been to acknowledge its contributions.

In 1902 the first independent public junior college in the country, Joliet Junior College, was established for students deemed academically and socially underprepared for university studies.

Morrill Land Grant Act made teaching and learning applied subjects such as business, agriculture, and technical programs a legitimate activity in higher education. The Act also extended access beyond the privileged few by guaranteeing admission to resident students from states that housed one of the new colleges (Brubacher and Rudy 1976). When these land grant institutions first opened, incoming freshmen—mostly 14-year-old boys—attended classes to learn basic reading, writing, and arithmetic skills since their schooling had been limited by a public education system that did not include high school (Maxwell 1979). Students could not take regular college courses until they completed a "battery of courses" in college preparatory departments (Boylan and Saxon 1998). Known as the "people's colleges," these new land-grant institutions were not for all, despite their popular name: they excluded minorities and limited opportunities for women, and within a decade, most would move to selective admissions based on academic merit or promise (Roueche and Roueche 1993). When this first Morrill Land Grant Act was passed, only three historically black colleges and universities (HBCUs) existed in the country. Despite their name, these early HBCUs mainly provided elementary and secondary schooling to black students who had very few or no opportunities to become educated.

When the Second Morrill Land Grant Act passed in 1890, states with racially segregated public higher education systems had to establish a land-grant institution for black students whenever a racially restricted land-grant institution was established for whites. Based on this requirement, sixteen black land-grant colleges were founded at border and southern states. These HBCUs mainly offered courses in agricultural, mechanical, and industrial subjects, not college-level courses and degrees (U.S. Department of Education 1991). In 1896, the U.S. Supreme Court's decision in *Plessy v. Ferguson* legitimized a "separate but equal" doctrine in public education and established two education systems for a racially divided public. The *Plessy* decision also called on HBCUs to provide training for black teachers who would teach in the segregated schools. The number of new land-grant institutions created throughout the country by the Second Morrill Act meant that more than half of the students admitted to higher education needed preparatory work.

A decade later, government-imposed admission quotas forced many higher education institutions to compete for students they did not really want. These "new" students were hardly tolerated at some institutions (Brier 1984). In 1902 the first independent public junior college in the country, Joliet Junior College, was established for students deemed academically and socially underprepared for university studies. By dividing four years into two distinct educational experiences, the junior college and the senior college, the "hordes" of high school students who wanted to continue their education could go directly to the junior college so universities could concentrate on preparing academically able and socially acceptable students for the professions (Zwerling 1976).

But even students who met universities' admission requirements still had difficulties. In 1926, when one half of the freshmen at a prestigious university did not meet course requirements and 16 percent failed all their courses (Wyatt 1992), William F. Book created a groundbreaking How to Study course.

Convinced that students' reading and study habits were the problem, not their lack of intelligence, he chose not to teach generic reading and study skills that clearly did not transfer to multiple content areas. Instead, he acknowledged the effort required to understand complex material, taught reading tied to disciplinary contexts, and expected students to use what they read in the world. Book also worked closely with students to develop study strategies that would help them overcome problems they experienced in their academic studies (Book 1927, cited in Roueche and Roueche 1993).

By 1929 the widespread introduction of general survey courses and lengthy reading assignments led to a proliferation of remedial reading clinics on many four-year campuses, including at Harvard in 1938; these clinics were modeled after their K-12 predecessors (Maxwell 1979). People taking pre-college-level courses, once referred to as "preparatory students," became known as "remedial students." While how-to-study courses of the day adopted some of Book's ideas, the new remedial reading courses did not follow his lead despite evidence supporting the success of his approach. Instead, generic skills such as skimming, scanning, and vocabulary development—severed from meaningful content— continued to be taught.

The remedial reading clinics also sought to increase students' reading rate by assigning eye movement and eye span exercises (Roueche and Roueche 1993), a practice still in use in some reading labs in higher education institutions in the 1980s. Established curriculum included a series of reading books, tied to K-12 grade levels, where students were timed on how long it took to read a brief passage, identical in length to all passages in the series. Their recorded time, combined with the number of questions about the passage answered correctly, "measured" reading readiness for college-level work. This approach that actively promotes surface learning and dissuades students and teachers from the more difficult work associated with reading for deep learning is still regarded, in some quarters, as an indicator of reading ability.

Fourteen years after Book created his How to Study curriculum, Mortimer Adler's classic 1940 guide, *How to Read a Book*, outlined how imaginative literature, history, science and mathematics, philosophy, and the social sciences ought to be read given their disciplinary logic. As Adler points out in the preface to a new issue of his book "to achieve all the purposes of reading, the desideratum must be the ability to read different things at different— appropriate—speeds, not everything at the greatest possible speed" (Adler and Van Doren 1972, x).

In the mid-1930s, the idea that junior colleges should serve community educational needs through the provision of comprehensive adult education programs laid the foundation for the community college movement (Roueche and Roueche 1993). In 1947, the Truman Commission on Higher Education called for the establishment of locally controlled colleges so all citizens regardless of race, sex, religion, geographical location, or financial condition could benefit from postsecondary education to the fourteenth grade; this declaration spurred on the community college movement. "Access to everyone who can profit from instruction" became a founding principle of community colleges. These

In the mid-1930s, the idea that junior colleges should s erve community educational needs through the provision of comprehensive adult education programs laid the foundation for the community college movement.

institutions, many established by citizens' movements and referred to as "democracy's colleges," attracted educators and community organizers who were prepared to work hard to democratize higher education. Highly publicized efforts to desegregate higher education, combined with growing international criticism of the treatment of African Americans, led to the inclusion of "race" in the list of factors that could no longer be a basis for excluding prospective students from higher education's new colleges.

This explicit reference to race marked another turning point in African Americans' long struggle, begun prior to the Civil War, for universal education as a necessary basis for freedom and citizenship. James D. Anderson notes that by 1866 more than five hundred schools existed in the Confederate states independent of and predating northern benevolent associations' involvement or aid; this network had been organized by the educational collectives associated with the freedmen educational movement (Anderson 1988, 6-15). Despite a long-standing commitment in African American communities to learning and self-improvement, Anderson's summary of the seventy-five-year period he studied bares a stark reality: "for the majority of black children in the South . . . not even public elementary schools were available. High schools were virtually non-existent, and the general unavailability of secondary education precluded even the opportunity to prepare for college" (285). When the "common schools crusade" from 1830 to 1860 made public elementary schools universally accessible to most American children, the exception was black children in the South who would not have any access to public elementary schools for another forty years until a "second crusade" occurred from 1900 to 1935. When American high schools were being transformed from elite private institutions to public schools from 1880 to the mid-1930s and the participation of high-school-aged children increased from less than 3 percent to 47 percent over a fifty-year period, southern local and state governments expanded the benefits of public secondary education only to white children. The very few black high schools that did exist were located in urban areas. As Anderson points out: "The treatment accorded black children during the transformation of American secondary education helps to disentangle general class discrimination from its more specific form of racial oppression. By the early 1930s, state-sponsored and state-funded building campaigns had made public secondary schools available to all classes of white children. Afro-Americans were generally excluded from the American and southern transformation of public secondary education" (187-88). This history explains how dramatic the victory was in 1935 when Thurgood Marshall, acting on behalf of the National Association for the Advancement of Colored People (NAACP), successfully challenged one university that refused to admit a student to its law school based on race. In 1938 NAACP won another similar case, the second of many more that would challenge segregation in graduate and professional schools.

During World War II, the SQ3R study and reading strategy,[3] still used currently in many campus reading and study skills labs, was developed to help servicemen enrolled in intensive eight-week courses retain information from college textbooks (Maxwell 1979). From 1944 to 1955, the G.I. Bill of Rights made it possible for millions of ex-servicemen to go to college, and programs such as General Educational Development (GED) or Grade 12 Equivalency became widespread. Counseling provided study skills courses, and English and mathematics departments provided basic skills or "refresher courses" designed specifically for veterans. These courses also enrolled students with proven ability in some academic studies who needed "remediation" only in a specific area of academic work (Boylan and Saxon 1998). As the numbers of veterans declined, government-funded reading and study skills centers, tutoring services, and counseling centers became institutionalized for all students' use (Maxwell 1979).

In the 1950s and 1960s, public universities combined selectivity with catch-up intersession and summer session preparation courses similar in design to those offered in the war years for able students who needed upgrading in a particular subject area (Roueche and Roueche 1993).

Organizing for civil rights throughout the 1950s and 1960s, specifically the campaign for an integrated school system from elementary, high school, and college to graduate and professional schools—along with the student movement for civil rights, had a profound impact on higher education and affected practice within developmental education. By 1950, NAACP decided to focus all legal battles on "obtaining education on a non-segregated basis" (Kluger 1975, 27). In December 1952, the Supreme Court heard five school segregation cases from South Carolina, Virginia, Delaware, the District of Columbia, and Kansas, consolidated under the name of one case, *Brown v. Board of Education of Topeka, Kansas*. In May 1954, the Supreme Court ruled unanimously, ". . . in the field of public education the doctrine of 'separate but equal' has no place. Separate educational facilities are inherently unequal" (Williams 1990, 131).

Most schools for blacks, though, "remained segregated with poorer facilities and budgets compared with traditionally white institutions" (U.S. Department of Education 1991, 3). This continued discrimination affected thousands of students. For instance, in 1953, public black colleges enrolled more than 43,000 students and around 32,000 more students were enrolled in smaller private colleges in the border and southern states and at HBCUs such as Fisk University, Hampton Institute, Howard University, Meharry Medical College, Morehouse College, Spelman College, and Tuskegee Institute. When Congress passed Title VI of the Civil Rights Act of 1964 to speed up the process of desegregating education by providing the means for ensuring equal opportunity in federally assisted programs and activities, racially segregated education systems still existed in nineteen states, a decade after the "separate but equal" doctrine was overturned.

The *Brown* Supreme Court decision followed by the Montgomery bus boycott and the active involvement of students in the Civil Rights Movement led Ella Baker, a grassroots organizer and the executive director of the Southern Leadership Christian Conference (SLCC), to call a conference for students in the spring of 1960 that would lead to the formation of an independent organization, the Student Non-Violent Organizing Committee. The student-led and organized sit-in movement, freedom rides, and literacy campaign that was part of the drive to register voters in the South became the inspiration for widespread student-led changes in higher education, among these the Open Admissions Movement in

Organizing for civil rights throughout the 1950s and 1960s, specifically the campaign for an integrated school system from elementary, high school, and college to graduate and professional schools— along with the student movement for civil rights, had a profound impact on higher education and affected practice within developmental education.

1970. This student activism—and the possibilities for equitable education—spilled into the academy. Many students, a number of whom would become teachers and developmental educators, were introduced to the critical and popular pedagogy associated with open education outside the academy[4] including Native American traditional practices, post-emancipation schools, workers' education programs, Highlander's integrated workshops, and the grassroots civil rights' Citizenship Schools along with international alternatives to formal schooling from literacy education in Brazil to folk schools in Denmark, study circles in Sweden, the frontier college in Canada, and the adult education movement in Britain.

Within higher education, community colleges and developmental education programs both accepted and assumed the responsibility for ensuring that these students, now described as "non-traditional," "disadvantaged," and/or "remedial," would be academically successful.

For prospective students and their families, higher education's accessibility is signaled by the *cost* of an education and the kind of financial aid available. The Higher Education Act of 1965 provided the financial means through Title IV aid[5] for educationally disadvantaged, low-income groups, minorities, and women to further their education. Within higher education, community colleges and developmental education programs both accepted and assumed the responsibility for ensuring that these students, now described as "non-traditional," "disadvantaged," and/or "remedial," would be academically successful. Equalization of opportunity expressed as an open door admissions policy ushered in what Cross (1976) refers to as the egalitarian, democratic era in higher education as compared to previous periods where access was based on merit or one's elite status.

In this period of promise, findings from the first national study of remedial education shocked educators. In the research report *Salvage, Redirection, or Custody?* (1968), John Roueche could find no evidence that developmental education programs did anything to remedy student deficiencies. Although he admired community colleges' commitment to "access for all," his research revealed that as many as 90 percent of students who placed in remedial courses withdrew or failed, even on campuses where the courses were required. Was the open door in fact a revolving door? Other critiques would soon follow tempered by civil rights and open admissions issues: some studies identified inequitable practices that tracked students by class, race, and ethnicity away from academics into vocational programs or left students to languish in the academy, without support, until they decided themselves that they did not belong (Karabel 1972; Zwerling 1976; Brint and Karabel 1989).

The push for open admissions was not restricted to community colleges despite a Carnegie Commission recommendation to this effect. In 1970, student protests resulted in the implementation of open admission programs at The City University of New York (CUNY). All New York City high school graduates were eligible to attend any one of the CUNY campuses regardless of their previous academic standing. CUNY became a lighting rod for critiques, among these charges that the curriculum was in danger of being dummied down and standards lowered. Yet CUNY's open-admission students, who tested substantially lower than regularly admitted students when they first arrived, after one year's work reached *at least* the verbal and mathematical skill levels attained initially by regularly admitted students (Rossman et al. 1975, cited in

Roueche and Roueche 1993, 123). Astin (1985) reviewed this study, confirmed its results, and drew attention to what developmental education practitioners already knew about most people in their classes: given appropriate resources and sufficient time, motivated yet underprepared students can develop the abilities to do college-level work.[6]

The CUNY results are all the more noteworthy in relation to the emerging consensus that new students did not "fit" easily into traditional practices, including those in developmental education: "remediation could not be approached by tackling poor study habits or teaching reading skills in isolation from other courses; the students were bringing an unbelievable variety of problems to the classroom that could not be addressed in a simplistic manner" (Roueche and Roueche 1993, 43). Practices historically associated with developmental education programs that served "privileged white males," then "mostly white males" turned out to be wholly inadequate for a new set of student subpopulations, "non-traditional women and men, and federal legislative priority groups such as first generation college students, economically-disadvantaged students, and students of color" (Arendale 2002, 16). Many developmental programs, faced with a wildly disparate group of adult learners, adopted a competency-based mastery model of instruction. Based on proficiency test results, students "placed" at a particular level in a series of self-paced modules. Most commercially purchased programs divided processes such as reading, writing, and mathematical reasoning/calculating into discrete, sequential skill and sub-skill exercises. Students did exercises, completed quizzes, and took unit tests within an assigned "level." If they reached mastery (85 percent of questions answered correctly), they moved on to the next "competency"; if not, they repeated a second version of the module.

Cross's concern about higher education's ineffectiveness in addressing the needs of "New Students," her critique of a deficiency conception and related compensatory programs, and her insistence that we pay attention to the kind of education offered to these students originate in this highly controversial time. Maxwell wrote her insider's account of developmental practice in the same period, "to fill the gap between liberals who eulogize the egalitarian goals of the college and conservatives who condemn all efforts to help students as 'spoon-feeding' and as 'failures'" (Cross 1979, xi).

By the end of the 1970s, most two-year and many four-year institutions in the country, compelled by a mix of legislation, government funding, and political pressure—most certainly the Civil Rights Movement followed by the Open Admissions Movement—opened their doors, or had them pried open, to accommodate an influx of students destined to become the next millennium's new majority on many campuses.

From a remedial to a developmental paradigm

In the 1970s, developmental educators, not immune to the debates of the day, began to articulate a new approach to working with underprepared students that did not focus narrowly on identifying "deficits" in students' academic backgrounds. Milton Spann Jr. and Suella McCrimmon note that faculty working

In the 1970s, developmental educators, not immune to the debates of the day, began to articulate a new approach to working with underprepared students that did not focus narrowly on identifying "deficits" in students' academic backgrounds.

The distinction, drawn with practitioners in mind, invites us to think more deeply about the process of learning and how we learn best.

with academically at-risk college students did not like the pejorative connotations associated with the term "remedial education" and began to replace it with another: "The term developmental . . . focused on the student's potential rather than the student's deficit. Since the goal of developmental education is a fully developed and fully functioning person, focusing on academic skills alone is insufficient if students are to make the transition to all-around effective students and involved citizens" (Spann Jr., and McCrimmon 1998, 41). As Boylan and Saxon indicate, the change was also predicated on the growing scholarship on human growth and intellectual and social development made known through the work of Piaget, Bruner, Kohlberg, and Perry:

> A variety of noncognitive or "developmental" factors . . . were also discovered to be of critical importance to academic success. These additional factors included such things as locus of control, attitudes toward learning, self-concept, autonomy, ability to seek help, and a host of other influences having nothing to do with students' intellect or academic skill. By the late 1970s, educators who worked with underprepared students developed an entirely new paradigm to guide their efforts. Instead of assuming that students were simply deficient in academic skills and needed to have these deficiencies remediated, they began to assume that personal and academic growth were linked—that the improvement of academic performance was tied to improvement in students' attitudes, values, and beliefs about themselves, others, and the educational environment . . . This new model involved the teaching of basic skills combined with assessment, advising, counseling, tutoring, and individualized learning experiences designed not just to reteach basic content, but also to promote student development. (Boylan and Saxon 1998, 7-8)

The changes Boylan and Saxon name correspond to a broader, holistic understanding of students' needs as described by Maxwell, Cross, and, in 1998 Martha Casazza.[7]

Cross clarifies what this shift represents for student learning by differentiating between the purpose of a remedial program, "to overcome academic deficiencies," and the purpose of a developmental program, "to give attention to the fullest possible development of talent and to develop strengths as well as to correct weaknesses" (1976, 31). The distinction, drawn with practitioners in mind, invites us to think more deeply about the process of learning and how we learn best. To return to Tagg's example of the toddler learning to walk, do we frame the toddler's fall as a basis for designing curriculum and instructional practice or do we frame the process of learning to walk, both falling down and getting up?

David Arendale's account of two innovative practices—Learning Assistance Centers and Supplemental Instruction—illustrates the difference between remedial and developmental perspectives. Both these initiatives, created at American universities in the early 1970s, quickly spread to other universities and community colleges throughout the country and internationally.

Arendale credits the Learning Assistance Center (LAC) model, developed by Frank Christ from California State University, Long Beach, with moving developmental programs away from a focus on remedial services for a subpopulation of remedial students toward a more comprehensive approach designed to enhance and enrich learning for all students on campus.[8] From the outset, in contrast to reading laboratories and academic support services of the day, Christ insisted on the comprehensive nature of LAC and its theory-based developmental orientation while "vigorously opposing any stigma that it was 'remedial' and only for inadequately prepared, provisionally admitted, or probationary students" (Christ 1997, 1-2, as cited in Arendale 2002, 17). It would be housed in one central and accessible facility, designed to meet multiple purposes: all students could use LAC resources including tutorial assistance and a library of basic study aids to get higher grades. The LAC would also be a referral service to helping agencies; a training center for paraprofessionals, peer counselors, and tutors; and a center for faculty development.[9]

The second example, Supplemental Instruction (SI), developed by Deanna Martin at the University of Missouri-Kansas City in 1973, targets high risk courses rather than students, a radical turnabout from a deficit approach (Martin and Arendale 1994). Without money to create a comprehensive LAC and in a state where four-year institutions were prohibited from providing developmental courses, Martin, a doctoral student in reading instruction, used data from a national survey of learning center directors to develop an approach that would avoid the common problems they named:

> Services were ancillary to the institution; standardized tests were insufficient to predict students who needed assistance; services were often provided too late to help students; students did not have time or money to enroll in additional developmental courses; students displayed difficulty in transferring study strategies to the academic content courses; individual tutoring was expensive; students often did not avail themselves of services for fear of being stigmatized; and evaluation of learning services was inadequate. (Arendale 2002, 18)

Martin shepherded a very different idea through the bureaucracy: target high-risk courses (those with a 30 percent or higher rate of D or F final course grades and course withdrawals, e.g., algebra, chemistry, anatomy) and recruit students who did well in the course to help incoming students. These able students would attend classes with new students, model good study habits, work with the instructor to identify key concepts and skills, and lead three or more regularly scheduled, out-of-class study sessions each week for all students enrolled. At these peer-facilitated sessions, students would discuss ideas related to the course and work collaboratively on problems and assignments. By 1983, the success of SI became known outside developmental education and outside the country.[10] By 1999, Arendale reported that within the United States, "more than a quarter million students participate in SI during each academic term . . . and research studies have consistently replicated the findings that SI is a cost effective program that contributes to increased academic achievement, persistence, and graduation rates" (Arendale 2002, 21).

Both of these initiatives, along with others, recast the role that developmental education—now alert to students' abilities and potential not their deficits—could play in the academy. Some campuses established comprehensive community-based continuing education, adult education, and developmental education programs from literacy up to college preparation that included well-articulated connections among basic skills instruction, English as a Second Language, life experience courses, and introductory college-level courses. Other campuses experimented with an abilities-based approach to teaching, learning, and assessment within broad skill areas such as critical thinking, reading, and writing across the curriculum, or within subject specific areas such as the sciences and mathematics. Faculty in composition and communication wrestled with how to restructure writing instruction with attention to issues of language and identity brought to the fore at CUNY during the open admissions era (Fox 1999; Kates 2001). By the mid-to-late 1980s, some community colleges and universities, often using SI and LAC, began to experiment with different learning community models within developmental education or between developmental education and college level studies.

Other campuses experimented with an abilities-based approach to teaching, learning, and assessment within broad skill areas such as critical thinking, reading, and writing across the curriculum, or within subject specific areas such as the sciences and mathematics.

Research-based best practices

After the disappointing results of the first 1968 national study where Roueche concludes that "intuition rather than research appears to be the basis for most remedial programs" (Roueche 1968, 42), evaluation of developmental programs began to replace anecdotal evidence. Within the developmental education field there is now a robust literature on research-based best practices (e.g., Boylan 2002; Casazza and Silverman 1996; McCabe 2000, 2003; Roueche and Roueche 1993; 1999).

In *High Stakes, High Performance: Making Remedial Education Work* the Roueches point out that successful programs for academically underprepared students "marry" two goals that critics argue are mutually exclusive—access and academic excellence (1999, 43). They invite institutions to study exemplary program models, adapt approaches to their campus circumstances, and evaluate their work based on explicitly stated aims and results achieved, not "efforts made." The Roueches emphasize a proactive institutional commitment to at-risk students' academic success as the following précis of their key recommendations and conclusions indicates.

a) *Provide a holistic approach to programs for at-risk students:* Successful programs involve intentional collaborative efforts from multiple areas of the campus including financial aid (tuition, support for child care, and transportation), counseling, and advising: "A successful learning lab, a strong reading program, or an excellent mathematics program, if offered as a stand alone instructional service or class, falls far short of the broader institutional commitment that colleges must make" (46).

b) *Abolish voluntary placement in remedial courses:* Successful programs assess entering students' academic abilities and, based on these results, ensure that students are academically prepared to do college-level work: " . . . motivation cannot replace missing or inadequate skill development, assessment tests are valid indicators of more serious deficiencies, and adulthood is not a 'free pass' to every course in the college curriculum" (48).

c) *Create a more seamless web:* Cooperation between sending and receiving institutions at critical transition points from high school to college, and community and technical colleges to four-year institutions are regarded as critical arenas for educational reform: " . . . direct interventions to provide support and direction should not be abandoned by one institution before they are assumed by another. Collaboration and strong linking mechanisms are critical to successful transition" (51).

These points are included in McCabe's recommendations to public decision-makers and community college leaders (2000a).

In *Accent on Learning*, Cross established early benchmarks for best practices in developmental classrooms based on a review of thirty years of research on working with underprepared students. She presented her findings as a series of recommendations for designing effective programs and curricula. Three key points underscore her recommendations, and these continue to surface in more current summaries of best practices. Like Book, Cross insists "skills training must be integrated into the other college experiences of the student." She supports this recommendation with overwhelming evidence that "transfer of training" does not occur automatically. Emphasizing theory- and research-based program design, she recommends that practitioners be flexible and open-minded about curricular and pedagogical practices until "more is known." She uses the example of skill development to underscore this point: "We do not even know which skills developed to what level are important to academic survival . . . " (Cross 1976, 42-45). Cross also argues that degree credit should be granted for remedial classes since this initial "reward" encourages student persistence.

In *What Works* (2002), Hunter Boylan summarizes the twenty-five-year period following the synthesis done by Cross. He defines "best practices" as the organizational, administrative, instructional, counseling, advising, and tutoring activities engaged in by highly successful developmental programs and names thirty-three distinct practices. Practitioners and educators knowledgeable about the field will recognize in his summary the broad contours on which the particulars of good teaching and learning are grounded.

Various research studies contribute to the picture that emerges. An outstanding feature of effective programs is an explicit developmental philosophy where the "whole" learner is placed at the center of practice; respect and empathy for learners is a central and unifying value (Casazza and Silverman 1996; Donovan 1974; Kiemig 1983). Exemplary programs challenge students. As Cross observed in *Beyond the Open Door* (1971), "the teacher who accepts poor performance (basically because he or she does not think the student can do better—or thinks that because of past injustices the student should not have to do better) is doing a grave disservice to New Students. In the final analysis, the teacher who cares must have enough teaching skill and enough confidence in the student to create the environment and situations that require the student's best

An outstanding feature of effective programs is an explicit developmental philosophy where the "whole" learner is placed at the center of practice; respect and empathy for learners is a central and unifying value.

Successful programs use trained peer tutors and integrate laboratories offering tutoring and self-paced computerized instruction with classroom activities . . .

efforts" (171). Effective programs integrate basic skill development with college-level materials (Maxwell 1979; Rouche and Rouche 1999; McCabe 2000a); students' critical thinking abilities are developed through reflective writing and critical reading (CQIN/APQC 2000). Successful programs use trained peer tutors and integrate laboratories offering tutoring and self-paced computerized instruction with classroom activities (Boylan et al.1992; McCabe 2000a). An adult learning environment, a committed staff knowledgeable about research on learning and learning problems, ongoing assessment of students' learning, systematic program evaluation, administrative support, and stable funding are also essential components of effective programs (Noel et al. 1985).

The quality of instruction has the most impact on students' academic performance (Boylan et al. 1992). In *What Works*, Boylan notes: "Instructors cannot control students' social or economic backgrounds nor can they have much influence on their work or home life. But they can control what is done in the classroom . . . quality of instruction refers not only to delivery methods but also to classroom organization, management, and environment" (2002, 68). Among the twelve models, methods, and techniques he identifies that contribute to the quality of instruction, "develop learning communities" tops the list of practices. The recognized advantages include: the mutual support a community offers its members (Astin 1993); increased retention and improved student grades (Tinto 1997); improved student attitudes toward learning (Tinto 1994); and dramatic increases in student persistence (McCabe and Day 1998). A number of the techniques and methods named in this instructional practices section are part of learning community pedagogy, among these the use of classroom assessment techniques and active collaborative learning strategies as well as the intentional development of students' critical thinking and analytical abilities. Other models named in this section invite practitioners to "use supplemental instruction" and "use mastery learning."

Missing from the acknowledged benefits of learning communities has been the hallmark of all learning community work: *integrative learning that is academically rigorous, engaging, and inclusive of all students' experience.* To realize this aim is the raison d'etre of learning community work more than improving retention and persistence, although these are welcome byproducts. In fact, current accounts of best practices in developmental education do not address curricular issues, the "what" of learning. If we recall Adelman's research, the intensity and quality of high school curriculum is the critical factor in students' successful transition from secondary school to college level work and eventual degree completion.[11] While developmental education programs do not base developmental curricula or instructional practices on a secondary school model, the pivotal importance of curriculum cannot be ignored. Within higher education, developmental education serves as an abbreviated and intense transition to college-level work—an academic apprenticeship, if you like, for people who need to develop the cluster of abilities and habits of mind associated with academic success. To reorient students' approaches to learning, which is the distinctive work of developmental education (Cross 1971), we need to be attentive to the "what" of learning; an education of quality is about *something.*

Shifting from deficit to research-based developmental curriculum

How do we know if students are appropriately prepared to do intellectually demanding work, a telling measure of a developmental program's effectiveness? Do students need to work on basic skills *before* they move on to demanding, substantive learning associated with college-level studies and learning communities or can students do both at the same time? These questions are not new but they focus attention on the shifting curricular and pedagogical ground that moving from a deficit to a developmental conceptual framework entails. Indeed, a current debate among developmental faculty at one Washington state community college on whether developmental students should participate in a book seminar planned for an entire campus brings to mind the bold decision that led to the *Declaration of Human Rights* becoming the core curriculum for Citizenship Schools. At this college, though, opposing views about students' participation is one of those flash points that can be especially illuminating if educators dare to broach the hard conversation on how we might prepare all students to participate fully and confidently in the intellectual and moral life of a community, at college and beyond.

Grubb and his colleagues, through their inside look at community colleges in *Honored But Invisible* (1999), established what good practice does *not* look like. In many developmental classrooms, curriculum that patronizes adult learners is still in place, from skill and drill exercises that numb the mind to workbooks full of trivial math problems, dull reading passages, and uninspiring writing assignments. Students keen to begin college-level work slog through curriculum that turns learning into pointless drudgery. Clearly, instructional practice lags behind research on learning and effective developmental education programs. Like other areas of the academy, we can find "best and worst" cases, but, as Maxwell observed twenty-five years ago, only the most capable students survive second-class learning. Whenever faculty development on research-based good practices is short-changed, students bear the cost.

From decontextualized skills to recontextualized abilities

From the perspective of a teacher, the shift from a deficit to a research-based developmental curriculum requires a fundamental rethinking of established practices, specifically a shift away from an emphasis on creating curriculum based on decontextualized skills to curriculum aimed at preparing students for college-level work where skillful learning is highly contextualized. Students need to develop the abilities associated with "learning how to learn" in multiple and varied contexts—a key learning goal of curriculum aimed at preparing students for college-level work.

Students who insist on knowing how the learning of generic skills will help them succeed at college prompt us to rethink established practice. The first students I taught in a developmental studies program in the early 1980s, demoralized by placement results indicating between fifth-to-eighth-grade reading levels, demanded to know how *this reading class* would help them succeed at college. My students' anxiety and outright anger about the placement tests as well as my previous experience teaching undergraduates in university settings and adults in community-based, popular education programs led us down

How do we know if students are appropriately prepared to do intellectually demanding work, a telling measure of a developmental program's effectiveness?

The Pedagogy of Possibilities: Developmental Education, College-Level Studies, and Learning Communities

I focused classroom work on a topic-based inquiry so the development of essential academic skills would occur in the context of learning something significant and substantive over time.

an experimental curricular track other than the competency-based mastery model that informed the existing reading curriculum. This teaching experience, briefly summarized below, illustrates one approach to designing a curriculum that brings students' existing abilities to the fore and "recontextualizes" them in relation to expectations associated with demanding college level work.

Since students in my class had very different career and educational goals in mind—and without the option of integrating this developmental class with a college-level course—I focused classroom work on a topic-based inquiry so the development of essential academic skills would occur in the context of learning something significant and substantive over time. My own undergraduate experience in an interdisciplinary program served as a source of inspiration as did my experience teaching sociology. Since students' engagement was critical, I decided to use a participatory research methodology to construct a curriculum that would focus on a contentious public issue that affected people's personal lives. The class chose the then impending free trade agreement between the United States and Canada. We brainstormed a list of questions people cared about from losing jobs to employment opportunities over time to the possible loss of indigenous industry and a national identity. Students collected and read articles on free trade from multiple perspectives and with varying degrees of reading difficulty; they wrote papers identifying arguments for and against free trade, worked out the math behind some predications, and came up with more questions for further inquiry. They sought out the views of experts and people they disagreed with and became recognized authorities among their friends. Toward the end of the semester, the class participated in a college-wide forum where they raised issues regarding the moral and ethical implications of free trade for underdeveloped countries before these concerns had become a matter of public debate.

By choosing a single topic for inquiry that bridged people's everyday lives and college learning, I hoped to convey both the challenge involved in doing intellectual work and to demystify how people actually learn a specialized vocabulary, become knowledgeable about issues, appreciate different perspectives, struggle with complex ideas, write about what they know, and so on. We paid attention to the skills and strategies students used, and experimented with different approaches that might be more effective. Students became engaged in a critical reflective inquiry about their own approaches to learning. We concluded that people become knowledgeable not because they are smarter than other people but because they study something in depth, in an intellectually disciplined way, in the company of others, with many opportunities for practicing skills that are a means for learning and collaborating on projects, not ends in themselves. The public evidence that these students knew more than other students in "real" college classes about a national issue tipped the balance in favor of learner agency and empowerment. They knew they could do college-level work because they had done college-level work.

The point in sharing this teaching experience is this: learning something substantive is appropriate for all learners if less confident students and their teachers figure out how students' abilities that are everywhere in evidence outside school can be "translated" to an academic context. A developmental perspective begins by analyzing students' existing abilities as readers, writers, thinkers, and users of mathematical reasoning. Recontextualizing complex abilities in an academic setting or activating often overlooked "prior knowledge" gives students a firmer foundation for further learning at college. This view is predicated on the assumption that people in developmental classes are able learners and thinkers outside the academy who, with practice, can become able learners in academic contexts (Gibbs 1992; Smilkstein 2002).

For high-risk students, a critical orientation to higher education includes developing the abilities required to intellectually navigate the multiple subcultures of the academy—an orientation that is as essential as one that helps students locate and use campus support services and learning resources. The challenge of how we can support students' efforts to become their *own* able translators and navigators is the essence of developmental work.

The attraction of pairing a developmental course with a course students struggle with offers developmental educators circumstances similar to those in which Book developed his successful How to Study course and the Supplemental Instruction model was created. The anticipated and actual difficulties students experience in their college studies "shapes" the curriculum.

From "inherited" practice to research-based pedagogy

Like other areas of the academy, many developmental education programs are slow to change even if established practices run counter to research and a program's effectiveness is questioned, as is the case with developmental reading courses. Here, the stakes are especially high since so many entering students do not read at college level. In *A Commentary on the Current State of Developmental Reading Programs*, Martha Maxwell notes that developmental reading courses have been impervious to change.[12] She refers to content analysis research that indicates that the more than 500 reading textbooks published since the 1890s tend to reproduce patterns of previous textbooks including an emphasis on skill instruction: comprehension, vocabulary, reading rate, and study skills. She asks, "If developmental courses give students nothing important to read about and nothing to write about that remotely resembles college work, how can they hope to improve?"(1998, 162).

Maxwell is not an advocate of forced placement in developmental classes where negative effects include decreased self-confidence, low morale, and increased dropouts, even though she acknowledges that many students need to improve their reading skills. If this is the goal, the numerous studies she cites indicate that developmental reading classes are ineffective. Unlike Adelman (1999) whose research also confirms this finding, Maxwell does not share his conclusion that students who place in developmental reading classes have comprehensive literacy problems that are best addressed at community colleges, not four-year institutions. Instead, she marshals evidence from a variety of studies, which shows that high-risk students who take mainstream courses have higher reading scores, retention rates, and better grades than their counterparts who take developmental reading courses. Ironically, students in mainstream classes *read* a lot more and in greater depth than they typically do in developmental reading classes. Maxwell also highlights research on

For high-risk students, a critical orientation to higher education includes developing the abilities required to intellectually navigate the multiple subcultures of the academy . . .

psycholinguistics and cognitive psychology that ought to lead to a rethinking of reading curriculum and instruction:

> Reading was thought to be a linear process so that one progressed from easier skills (such as reading for facts) to the more complex skill of critical reading. We know now that reading is discipline-specific and skills learned in one genre may not transfer to other academic fields . . . Most authorities no longer believe that meaning lies in the text and that the teacher's job is to see that students understand the author's meaning. Psycholinguistic theory argues that reading and writing are modes of learning and share common purposes and processes. That is, they are ways that students construct meaning or ways of thinking and knowing. Reading involves an interaction between a learner's prior knowledge, text, and context; reading and writing are viewed as a single act of literacy that should be taught together. (Maxwell 1998, 160)

"Historically, the most successful model for high risk students who enter college with limited reading skills involves a core of intensive, interdepartmental courses that are team-taught and include reading, writing, mathematics and a mainstream course, usually in social science"

Maxwell is clearly in favor of pairing developmental reading and developmental writing courses but she also emphasizes curricular integration that is consonant with a learning community approach to developmental education: "Historically, the most successful model for high risk students who enter college with limited reading skills involves a core of intensive, interdepartmental courses that are team-taught and include reading, writing, mathematics and a mainstream course, usually in social science" (163). As in her 1979 guide, Maxwell continues to call for counseling to be integrated into this core as well as adjunct and Supplemental Instruction courses.

Addressing fragmented curriculum

Greater Expectations identifies the fragmentation of the curriculum as an especially daunting "barrier to quality" and the first-class learning envisioned for all students (2002, 16). Curricular coherence, a longstanding issue throughout higher education, is one that the Roueches (1999) also emphasize when evaluating developmental programs.

The sheer numbers of students attending college, their diversity, and chaotic attendance patterns exacerbate an old problem—one where a fragmented curriculum leaves students patching together an undergraduate education based on disconnected but available courses. The added factor is that today's students are on the move from institution to institution, taking courses in the traditional classrooms and online, with sometimes long interruptions between attending school and leaving. What are the possibilities of acquiring an education of quality in this highly atomized system where the division of knowledge into distinct fields is only one complaint? Less confident students often retreat from continuing college when faced with so many choices that do not seem to "go anywhere." Or, they gravitate to professional and technical programs that are internally coherent but have high dropout rates in threshold courses and low pass rates throughout the program.

The call for curricular coherence occurs in the context of a broad aim, a seamless education of quality for all students from kindergarten to graduate studies. To even articulate a developmental "education of quality"[13] that is embraced by an entire campus is an ambitious project—the equivalent of designing an integrative curriculum for the kind of "Learning Paradigm College" (2003) Tagg envisions. We turn briefly to one approach that is integral to designing learning communities from a developmental perspective; this approach invites us to examine what students are learning "in here" (developmental classes) in relation to requirements "out there" (intended programs and courses and/or the world outside the academy).

Articulating the developmental stages of an undergraduate education

The basis for collaboratively identifying "a developmental sequence . . . the kingpin of developmental theory" (Cross 1976, 158) is faculty expertise about students' learning based on an analysis of students' work. The language of designing curriculum—the difference between what we want students to know and be able to do and what they already know and do—is drawn from an influential paradigm in education, pioneered by Alverno College faculty (1994) and founded on a developmental and abilities-based approach to teaching, learning, and assessment.

The work of Alverno, a four-year urban college for women in Milwaukee, Wisconsin, is not mentioned in the developmental education literature on best practices even though what characterizes exemplary developmental programs is practiced not only in its College Transition Program but also throughout Alverno. Moreover, by far the majority of Alverno's students—mature adults with busy lives, many of whom did not complete high school and 38 percent of whom are from minority communities—would be tagged "high risk" with little if any chance of success. At Alverno most of these students meet the college's high expectations and graduate, a number continue their studies, and many are active in their communities.

Tim Riordan, one co-author of *Working with Underprepared Students* (Cromwell et al. 2003), offers an insight into Alverno's developmental philosophy by describing his experience when he bought his first computer. He knew what a computer was and he had worked on one, but the questions and comments of a helpful salesperson were in a language he didn't understand. "In effect," he writes, "I was 'underprepared' and I felt totally inept, even embarrassed." Riordan compares his experience to that of students new to his discipline, philosophy, where a short story or a novel is often a better way to introduce students to philosophical questions than explicit philosophical texts. Achieving facility with a discipline is a developmental process where students acquire a specialized language, knowledge, habits of mind, and the ability to *practice* the discipline over time: "One of our educational assumptions at Alverno is that learning is a developmental process and that our design and practice of teaching should reflect that."

The essence of Alverno's educational work is expressed in the college's mission: the personal growth and intellectual development of each person. This collective responsibility and mission applies to all students, no matter the skills and abilities they bring to college. In turn, incoming students know "learning how to learn is a serious part of student work" (ibid.).

The language of designing curriculum—the difference between what we want students to know and be able to do and what they already know and do—is drawn from an influential paradigm in education . . .

Alverno arrived at its distinctive abilities-based approach by way of a financial crisis in the late 1960s and the wisdom of its then president, Sister Joel Read, who believed the college could reinvent itself. She set aside time for people to meet every Friday afternoon to address two questions: As a community, what do we want Alverno graduates to know and be able to do in the world? What practices from your discipline/program are indispensable to the kind of undergraduate education imagined? This casting of education into the world led to the naming of eight generic abilities and, over time, the development of a culture where students learn to accurately self-assess these abilities in relation to explicit criteria and standards, and received feedback from faculty, peers, and external assessors (Alverno College Faculty 2000). Assessment and self-assessment continues throughout the undergraduate years as students reach levels associated with beginning, developing, and then advanced learning, Alverno faculty's supportive language for distinct stages of accomplishment.

An adaptable developmental model for designing curriculum

Countless faculty from schools, colleges, and universities—including many developmental educators—have worked with their own course materials at Alverno's Summer Institutes to figure out how to recast teaching and assessment practices using a developmental framework. The multi-layered, developmental model used by Alverno College faculty serves as a reference point.

Like all highly contextualized and successful models, though, the approach is based on an analysis of Alverno's own students' learning. For instance, the descriptors for beginning, developing, and advanced work are what interdisciplinary teams of Alverno faculty who serve in one of eight across-the-curriculum ability groups regard as the developmental stages in their students' learning; discipline groups also articulate a developmental sequence in relation to their students' ability to understand and use disciplinary knowledge. While details are not transferable to other campus cultures, Alverno's developmental approach is not limited to working with underprepared students nor do faculty imagine that students will only experience difficulties in their first year at college. Among the key features of Alverno's developmental perspective, the following are especially significant for designing integrative learning opportunities for developmental and other students.

a) *Make expectations for student learning explicit:* Alverno's curriculum is articulated in relation to over-arching abilities or expectations for graduates. In turn, these are embedded in expectations for the majors and professional/technical degrees. Here, the naming and articulation of expectations is the critical factor. The question *what do we want students to know and be able to do at the end of a developmental program or a course or a learning community* focuses thinking on key conceptions, abilities, habits of mind, skills, and attitudes that are valued.

b) *Build on students' existing abilities*: Abilities-based learning invites an analysis of students' existing abilities, the foundation for new learning. In the context of developmental education, we are interested in *what someone knows what to do as a reader*, *as a writer*, and *as a user of mathematics in their everyday lives*. Effective developmental curriculum and teaching map new learning onto students' existing abilities that at first glance do not 'fit' academic culture. Assessment at the outset is crucial.

c) *Identify beginning, developing, and advanced performance*: The distinctions Alverno uses to articulate developmental stages in learning stand in sharp contrast to a deficit model. What differentiates beginning work from developing work and this work from advanced work or, for instance, reading and writing in upper-level developmental courses as compared to college entry-level courses? What in our teaching and assessment practices create conditions for students to "move" from one developmental stage to the next? An examination of students' actual work by faculty determines these distinctions.

Self-assessment is a critical component of learning how to learn.

d) *Teach students to self-assess their learning*: Students' practice of self-assessment and self-reflection, a motivator for learning, is also developmental at Alverno. For instance, the importance of learning goals such as the "use of feedback" and "commitment to improvement" is reinforced within a campus culture that regards assessment as student learning. To move from a fear of external evaluation to learning motivated by one's own accurate self-assessment represents a fundamental shift toward independent, empowered learning. What are the conditions that support this kind of learner agency? Self-assessment is a critical component of learning how to learn.

e) *Develop assignments where students need to use what they know*: A distinction made by faculty between *possessing knowledge* and *using knowledge* focuses attention on evidence of learning that is "authentic"; students use what they know in "real" situations. For instance, the ability to take notes in lectures is developed by attending lectures, taking notes, and using these notes to do a "practice" in-class quiz. Math is more deeply understood through practical application and problem-based learning where numbers, for instance, are tied to a state's economic forecast, proposed budget cuts, and related tuition increases—an opportunity for students to become knowledgeable about decisions that affect their well-being and that of their families and communities.

The generative power of a developmental perspective is further illustrated by the example of a faculty-directed statewide project to identify faculty expectations related to reading, writing, mathematics, student responsibility, observing, listening, and speaking. The *College-Ready Project* in Washington state involves developmental and college level faculty from thirty-two community and technical colleges. One data source included a faculty survey based on the heuristic, "what should students know and be able to do." The responses from approximately 950 instructors who teach college-entry courses led to the development of a framework that outlines college-ready abilities or strategies. The project has evolved to include creating rubrics for assessing outcomes, designing assessments, and collecting faculty assignments and students' work.[14]

We will return to how a developmental and abilities-based approach to teaching and assessment can inform the design of learning communities in a subsequent discussion of learning community models. For now, we note that adopting a developmental perspective on learning throughout the academy welcomes and makes room for underprepared learners; it builds on students' existing abilities and assets; it renders obsolete the language of deficits and exclusion. It also compels us to act on the charge of our times: to find ways to include differently prepared students in demanding college level learning environments with the support they need to be successful. The next chapter hones in on this question.

Endnotes

1. See Smith, et al. forthcoming, for a history of the policy debates in this area in the last twenty-five years.
2. The National Association for Developmental Education defines developmental education as "any organized collection of courses and/or services designed to help underprepared students succeed." See its website for a more detailed definition of developmental education as a field of practice and research within higher education http://www.nade.net.
3. SQ3R is an acronym for a five-step reading strategy: survey or overview text, question, read, (w)rite, review.
4. See *Roots of Open Education in America* (1976), Ruth Dropkin and Arthur Tobier, eds., which also includes personal accounts of Yiddish schules, settlement houses, residential schools, the first day-care programs, and Early Progressive Schools.
5. Title IV student aid programs are founded on the premise that family members (the student, the student's spouse, and parents) have the primary responsibility to pay for higher education to the extent of their ability to pay.
6. See Phyllis van Slyck's current account of LaGuardia Community College-CUNY's New Student House program for at-risk incoming students in Section Two.
7. Casazza discusses the implications for student learning of other developmental theorists' work such as Freire, Vygotsky, Bruffee, Mezirow, and Baxter-Magolda.
8. For example the current National Association for Developmental Education (NADE) motto reflects a conception of developmental education that is not bound by a single department or particular group of students: "developmental education helps underprepared students prepare, prepared students advance, and advanced students excel."
9. LACs also provided a rationale for housing, under one roof, the multiple small-grant support programs created for students after the 1960s civil rights legislation.
10. In 1981, SI became certified as an Exemplary Educational Program by the U.S. Department of Education based on two criteria: improved academic achievement, i.e., students participating in SIs consistently received higher course grades; and improved student behaviors and attitudes, i.e., specifically lower withdrawal rates from target classes and higher rates of

persistence toward graduation. In the United Kingdom, SIs are known as Peer Assisted Learning (PAL) and in Australia, Peer Assisted Study Sessions (PASS). See http://www.umkc.edu/cad/si.

11. Many students in developmental classes missed high school curriculum because they were assigned to special classes; often, their preferred learning mode was not part of teachers' instructional repertoires.

12. Maxwell is a reading specialist; the first university English course she taught in the late 1940s was called "Reading Improvement" (Maxwell 1979).

13. See *Greater Expectations* (2002, 33) for a succinct account of the learning desired and related "facilitating strategies."

14. This project is co-led by developmental faculty members Teresa Massey and Pam Dusenberry. For more information contact project coordinator, Anna Sue McNeill, amcneill@sbctc.ctc.edu.

Chapter 3
Creating Supportive and Challenging Learning Environments:
The Learning Community Experience

Knowledge emerges only through invention and re-invention, through the restless, impatient, continuing, hopeful inquiry human beings pursue in the world, with the world, and each other.

Paulo Freire,
Pedagogy of the Oppressed

This chapter introduces the essentials of a learning community approach. We discuss various learning community models designed by faculty and academic staff for underprepared students that respond to issues raised in previous chapters. Thumbnail accounts of successful programs illustrate how learning communities can be both supportive and challenging for students new to higher education and academic work. They counter fragmented curricula, student disengagement, and faculty isolation, three factors that undermine efforts to provide an education of quality. Then, we turn to research on the impact of learning communities on student learning and what students say about their experience.

Learning communities link or cluster classes during a given term, often around an interdisciplinary theme or question, that enroll a common cohort of students.

Defining learning communities

The expression "learning community" has been used to describe people learning together in a classroom, in a residential hall, across a campus, and in an entire town. As we use it, "learning communities" refers to a variety of approaches to curricular reform that departs from the usual pattern of teachers teaching separate classes in separate subjects to separate groups of students. Learning communities link or cluster classes during a given term, often around an interdisciplinary theme or question, that enroll a common cohort of students. This represents an intentional restructuring of students' time, credit, and learning experiences to build community among students, among students and their teachers, and to build curricular connections.[1]

Learning communities vary from an integrative one- or two-credit seminar taken with two or more courses over a semester or quarter up to a full-time, one- or two-year program of integrated study. Campus models include freshmen interest groups, learning clusters, coordinated studies, interdisciplinary studies, federated learning communities, paired or linked courses, and wholly new inventions as well as a combination of models that may include linked assignments.[2] All these curricular designs are adaptable to the particular circumstances of any campus, the needs of its students, and faculty strengths and interests. Any of these models can have residence life components, other co-curricular components such as community-based service learning, and activities such as going on field trips, organizing potluck dinners, attending cultural events, and facilitating a campus-wide book seminar.

Learning communities vary based on degrees of curricular integration and the amount of collaboration among faculty; they also vary in terms of who teaches them, often involving full- and part-time faculty, counselors, student affairs professionals, and librarians. Sometimes advising, counseling, library research, reading and study skills, and tutoring in writing, mathematics, and the sciences are part of learning communities. Whatever the combinations, the aim is to foster explicit social and intellectual connections among people and ideas. At their best, all versions of learning communities practice pedagogies of active engagement and reflection, and students learn how to collaborate and take responsibility in the learning process.

Collaborative learning reframes the student role by requiring students to shift from a passive, privatized, and competitive learning mode to active, public, and cooperative ways of working.

Centrality of peer group

Learning communities promise students something very special—friendship through scholarship.[3] They build on the social nature of learning and proven power of the peer group to encourage student engagement (Astin 1993). Almost all public accounts of learning communities allude to this aspect of the learning community experience. For instance, De Anza Community College in Northern California, recognized for its distinguished work in ESL and developmental education (McCabe 2003; Roueche and Roueche 1999), introduces its Learning in Communities (LinC) program to students in this way: "The purpose of Learning Communities is to promote the success of our students by offering a better way to learn. We learn naturally by making connections between different ideas and experiences. In Learning Communities, we integrate two or more subjects to create a better and easier understanding of both. You work with the same community of students in the linked classes, helping each other succeed and making friends along the way. With some common readings and assignments, you learn more and complete more units with less stress."[4] Many learning communities also involve peer mentoring and other forms of students teaching students.

Centrality of collaborative learning

One of the core pedagogies[5] associated with learning community programs is active and collaborative learning. Like learning communities, "collaborative learning" is an expression that resonates with many educators because it recasts learning as a social and interactive activity. Jean MacGregor (1990) traces collaboration in education to the work of Dewey, Piaget, and Vygotsky who developed some of the basic tenets of experiential learning and emphasized the teacher's role in creating contexts for students to discover, construct, and reconstruct their understanding of the world. As MacGregor indicates, various communities of practice have enriched an understanding of collaborative learning, among these the cooperative learning movement, disciplinary-based strategies for peer learning especially in mathematics and writing, and problem-based approaches to learning.

Collaborative learning reframes the student role by requiring students to shift from a passive, privatized, and competitive learning mode to active, public, and cooperative ways of working. Group work often depends on individual reading, preparation of questions, and reflective writing *before* class. Because attendance affects group work, it is not a strictly personal matter. As MacGregor notes

> Many students . . . have difficulty accepting that collaborative learning with peers is real learning and has value, so conditioned are they to expecting teachers to be the sole source of knowledge in the classroom. Moreover,

there are the risks inherent in the public nature of collaborative work. Such work almost always entails talk, and a great deal of it. Learning collaboratively, students are working out loud, and the learning is "live"—on the air, as it were, bloopers and all. (1990, 26)

Dualistic and beginning thinkers (Perry 1970) often experience the most discomfort when teachers and texts are no longer viewed as authoritative. Perhaps student unease with this approach may explain why Hunter Boylan, who names learning communities as a best-practice instructional strategy within developmental education, voices this caution: "They are not for everyone in spite of the research documenting their success; some developmental students learn best in traditional courses" (2002, 70). Boylan includes this point under "tips," but offers no further elaboration. On the other hand, staying with students' preferences that reinforce passive approaches to learning and a tendency to repeat the learning of what is already known, does not serve well students who aspire to a college education, a point Cross makes in her portrait of the learner as a weak swimmer. Collaborative learning is not education as usual; it introduces community expectations into the classroom equation and alters the role of the teacher.

Paulo Freire's "banking conception of knowledge" is often cited to explain how interactive collaborative learning differs from a teaching-student relationship where teachers narrate or "tell" and students mechanically listen and memorize the narration. In the narrative education model, minds are containers to be filled, the places for deposits. Teachers do the depositing. Good teachers deposit more; good students take in more, an approach similar to a quantified conception of knowledge that is described in the research literature on deep learning. As Freire observes:

> In the banking conception of knowledge, knowledge is a gift bestowed by those who consider themselves knowledgeable upon those whom they consider to know nothing. Projecting an absolute ignorance onto others, a characteristic of the ideology of oppression, negates knowledge and education as processes of inquiry. The teacher presents himself to his students as their necessary opposite; by considering their ignorance absolute, he justifies his own existence. The students, alienated like the slave in the Hegelian dialectic, accept their ignorance as justifying the teacher's existence—but, unlike the slave, they never discover that they educate the teacher.
>
> The *raison d'etre* of libertarian education, on the other hand, lies in its drive towards reconciliation. Education must begin with the solution of the teacher-student contradiction, by reconciling the poles of the contradiction so that both are simultaneously teachers *and* students. (1970, 53)

Freire replaces the banking conception of knowledge with a model that sees knowledge as socially and culturally constructed. The epigraph for this chapter

Collaborative learning is not education as usual; it introduces community expectations into the classroom equation and alters the role of the teacher.

It is common to coordinated

studies, to clusters and linked

courses, and to federated

learning communities,

to put people together

and give them time and space—

real time and space—

to learn from each other.

illustrates the difference: "knowledge emerges only through invention and re-invention, through the restless, impatient, continuing, hopeful inquiry human beings pursue in the world, with the world, and each other" (1970). For Freire, collaborative learning is both pedagogy and epistemology. His views on education and teaching-and-learning apply to all learners—beginning, developing, and advanced. They originated from his teaching experience in an adult-education and literacy program he created for workers and peasants in an impoverished region in northeast Brazil, near Recife, where he grew up.

An active stance toward the world such as the one Freire describes is founded on a deep appreciation for what significant differences among people and communities of people imply for informed action in a world of extraordinary multiplicity.

Centrality of attending to diversity

Patrick Hill shares Freire's views on the social and cultural construction of knowledge. A member of the faculty at The Evergreen State College, Hill[6] recognizes that the organizational structures of the academy influence the teaching and learning process, fragmenting curriculum and often failing to promote learning as a social process and source of knowledge. In a speech given at Washington Center's Inaugural Conference on Learning Communities, during his tenure as provost, Hill introduced the underlying rationale for learning communities:

> . . . the fundamental structural move is to link related enterprises and to make structural changes which release, for faculties and students, the powers of human association. Dewey, among other people, has stressed that in our individualistic age we have forgotten about the powers of human association—what happens when you put people together. For example the stimulation of thought, the exposure to diversity, the need to clarify one's thinking in the community . . .

> It is common to coordinated studies, to clusters and linked courses, and to federated learning communities, to put people together and give them time and space—real time and space—to learn from each other. You are releasing the capacity of people to learn from each other, and it is as simple as that, what we are after . . . If you create those opportunities and make them real, and reward them, then a tremendous gush of creativity comes forth and people start to learn again, and to feel excited about their work. (1985, 4-5)

For Hill, the "exposure to diversity" is critical to authentic collaborative learning. In a later article for *Change* magazine, again on the rationale for learning communities, Hill extends community to mean a place or process by which diverse others engage in "conversations of respect" (1991, 41).

Hill has developed a variety of classroom practices that introduce new students to what he regards as their essential work at Evergreen, learning how to collaborate. In a recent lecture at the beginning of the fall 2003 quarter, Hill asks, "why are there such diverse opinions in the world? How come talking doesn't help us reach one opinion?" He weaves an Evergreen expectation—learning across significant differences—with insights drawn from the parable of the elephant and six blind men (who each know something different and partial about the elephant) to illustrate complex ideas related to the social and cultural construction of knowledge and the hard work that sustains authentic collaboration. He explains how each person in the yearlong coordinated studies program will be thinking, questioning, and actively learning from others. Students will write reader response papers based on a common book: each person will identify four or five meaningful passages that they want to talk about and one thing "that would make me want to throw the book across the room if I was the kind of person who I desperately am trying not to be." Teams of five students will meet to take turns reading their response papers; everyone will listen without comment. Later students will listen, without comment, to their teammates' responses to their paper. These weekly team meetings model attentive listening, the indispensable preparation for a seminar where the aim is to construct knowledge through dialogue. For Hill, conversations of respect are an intentional and learned practice.[7] Participants' experience and insights will be intrinsic to the knowledge the group constructs—its common property.[8]

William Koolsbergen describes two pedagogical practices associated with collaborative learning as a distinctive epistemology. A professor of humanities at LaGuardia Community College who teaches in thematically-linked liberal arts clusters and the developmental program's New Student House, Koolsbergen notes that in his oral communication class where thirty of thirty-five students will be from different cultural groups, students use their own often contradictory and diverse personas to appreciate how social roles are constructed and apprehended. He recounts how this new perception opens the door to learning from others' experience and cultural knowledge:

> Diversity is more than ensuring that our classes reflect a diversity of texts to reflect the diversity of our students. In learning communities especially, "doing" diversity means engaging in dialogue, confronting, and grappling with our diverse personas. Students are asked to engage in a variety of roles each day. Our students are workers, parents, children, non-native speakers, and retirees. They also come from culturally diverse backgrounds. Often they play multiple roles at one time when their work, family, language, and learning intersect. The class discussion is about how we construct these personas or have them assigned to us; the sensitivity to diversity follows as we deconstruct these social roles and look at what positive and negative attributes we attach to them. Because learning communities are designed by faculty from different disciplines who come together to find a way to approach teaching and learning through the different perspective of the disciplines, they are the ideal structure for dealing with diversity. (Koolsbergen 2001, 26)

Koolsbergen explains how faculty and students in the learning cluster learn how to engage in discussions that will move into unchartered territory. In their first scheduled hour together at the beginning of the semester, all faculty in the

Because learning communities are designed by faculty from different disciplines who come together to find a way to approach teaching and learning through the different perspective of the disciplines, they are the ideal structure for dealing with diversity.

teaching team meet all the students; they discuss the syllabi and the process for collaborative work (group formation, task examination, discussion, and reporting out). At the second meeting the students actively develop the "ground rules for discussion of diversity" for their community: rules are named, listed, discussed, voted on, and then copied down by one member and everyone signs the covenant, including faculty. Rules may include expected ones such as "create a safe atmosphere for open discussion," "assume that people do the best they can," and "combat stereotypes . . . that prohibit group cooperation and success," but others speak to institutionalized forms of oppression based on race, class, gender, sexual orientation, and the fact that we are "all systematically misinformed about our own group and about members of other groups" (26). The agreement not to blame but to educate rests on participants' understanding of the partiality of one's knowing and experience.

Phyllis van Slyck describes how she is redefining curriculum and pedagogy so students will *not* use their own experience as a frame of reference for understanding the world. van Slyck, a professor in the English department at LaGuardia who also teaches basic skills writing classes, uses Mary Louise Pratt's notion of the "contact zone," a space "where cultures meet, clash and grapple with each other"[9] as a starting place to teach a greater diversity of world literatures:

> . . . our curriculum and pedagogy must acknowledge that in many American colleges today we are educating students who have come from *many* different cultures, whose experiences and identities define them as potential citizens of the world. Contact zones must therefore be defined more broadly as spaces where diverse world literatures, and the cultures they represent and critique, may be taught in thematically organized contexts. (van Slyck 1997, 154)

Curricular choices, which intentionally introduce nonwestern experiences, language, and values into the classroom space, disturb what people *know* to be true. A comparative dialogue that uses western and nonwestern texts expands participants' cultural literacy. As van Slyck notes:

> We are . . . [not] required to become immediate "experts" on the cultures in question, not does it mean that we should teach irresponsibly without researching a particular area; rather, it means that we should begin to define our pedagogy around a more democratic and multicultural model of collaborative research, reflection, discovery, and decentering. (154)

van Slyck's account of repositioning herself and her students in this contact zone is grounded in the particulars of texts read, students' diverse reactions, and her commitment to moving students beyond an easy dismissal of others' experiences. She is learning to recast discussion questions and writing assignments to privilege comparative analysis: "I asked students to find examples of cultural and religious traditions which reflect commitment and responsibility to a particular culture (birth, death, and other rite of passage ceremonies in both western and nonwestern culture share this commitment) and to compare them . . . what are the purposes of these traditions? What values do they teach? Why is it important to teach respect for community? What would we lose if we gave this up? Can cultures accommodate both individual and communal values?" (157). The aim is to create a space for dialogue to occur where differences are explored: "Students may ultimately reject a particular practice, but they have learned the difference between an *informed* rejection and a naíve or unreflective one" (167). Her experience is that *all* students can meet the challenge of engaging in comparative cultural analysis and ethical negotiations and that all students can break with essentialist and monocultural notions of "truth."

The accounts of Hill, Koolsbergen, and van Slyck represent the kind of in-the-world, self-reflective learning that many learning communities encourage. Karen Spear (2003) puts it this way: "What remains constant is that learning communities are, at their core, a liberalizing and humanizing force in a student's education . . . while democracy need not be a *subject* of study, democracy becomes a *practice* of study within learning communities" (19). The creation of knowledge is a democratic, inclusive practice.

The impulse to turn the classroom into a place where democracy and education meet reflects a long tradition. The first learning community at the University of Wisconsin in 1927, created by philosopher and educational leader Alexander Meiklejohn, was designed to help students develop a unified scheme of reference to participate in the evolving American experience with democracy. They developed this through a two-year interdisciplinary program focused on democracy where students studied the classics and engaged in intensive dialogues on what it means to be a citizen.[10] Meiklejohn's colleague, John Dewey, a major force in educational reform in America and another major influence on learning community work, also saw schools as the site for developing the values and critical intelligence necessary for active participation in democratic community life.

At their best, learning communities help students develop a healthy skepticism about sure, confident knowledge, including their own. When learning is purposeful, framed by a question, theme, or issue that is sufficiently compelling and perplexing, the response is to actively seek out different perspectives and worldviews than those we know. Learning communities promote this kind of challenging learning; they try to support students in their efforts to develop an active stance toward the world, a sense of personal empowerment and personal responsibility, an ability to work with others, and an ability to deal with change, ambiguity, and complexity. These values need to be an essential feature in today's higher education curriculum, from developmental education to graduate studies.

At their best, learning communities help students develop a healthy skepticism about sure, confident knowledge, including their own.

Creating effective learning communities

Where learning communities are established on campus, the kind of models adopted, and the ways a teaching team works to combine courses into an integrated curriculum vary from campus to campus. We describe some of the approaches different campus teams have found helpful in either starting learning community work or scaling up existing initiatives: first, we identify key factors to consider when establishing learning communities for developmental students; second, we review three basic models that campuses typically adapt to their circumstances; third, we introduce a method for determining which model fits the degree of curricular integration and collaboration desired; and, fourth, we offer a condensed guide to the campus learning community examples that follow, organized according to research-based best practices in developmental education discussed in Chapter Two.

Locating developmental learning communities where student need is greatest

The location of learning communities within the institution depends on the goals for a learning community initiative—for students, for faculty, for the curriculum, and for the institution. Savvy innovators connect learning communities to the external communities their campus serves, their institution's distinctive mission and goals, existing educational innovations on the campus, and faculty strengths and interests.

Learning communities are sited throughout the academy—in developmental studies, freshmen/first-year initiatives, minors or majors, and graduate school programs; as strategies for coherence in general education and in across-curriculum initiatives such as writing, critical thinking, and quantitative reasoning;[11] and at transition points in undergraduate education from developmental to college-level work or from two- to four-year institutions. Many learning community programs focus on the critical first term or first year in college where the adjustment and developmental needs of entering students are greatest and the drop out rates are highest.[12] Most of these programs are designed so students can develop core academic skills in reading and communications, mathematics, and the sciences.

Learning communities for developmental students need to be intentionally located in the curriculum using the same approach as the Supplemental Instruction model previously discussed, the most effective intervention strategy in developmental education (Boylan 2002). The first step is to use data from institutional research to target "high risk" areas in the academy where students experience the most difficulty. These trouble spots include:

- high-risk courses where 30 percent of the students drift away after one month
- graveyard courses where 50 percent of the students earn low grades or drop out
- gateway courses that have a reputation among students for being tough
- platform courses for entry into professional and technical programs
- transition courses for developmental students and second-language speakers moving into liberal arts and professional/technical programs

The second step is to be attentive to patterns among students who are considered to be "at risk" in higher education: do students earn the credits they sign up for? Are some courses taken more than once and by a particular group of students?

Many learning community programs focus on the critical first term or first year in college where the adjustment and developmental needs of entering students are greatest and the drop out rates are highest.

Are some racial and ethnic groups underrepresented in some courses but overrepresented in others? For instance, Vauhn Wittman-Grahler (2002), who was teaching math in a racially-diverse institution noted that in her Calculus II class 100 percent of the students were white males compared to her developmental math class which averaged about 75 percent non-Asian students of color and an equally high percentage of women students. The third and final step is to share results with advisors, counselors, and tutors to find out if the data reflects their experience regarding courses and curriculum that pose the most difficulties for students.

While many learning communities initially form based solely on the interests of two or more faculty rather than areas of student need, learning communities for students who are already at risk in higher education need to be located in curricular trouble spots. Although curriculum restructuring begins here, this starting point does not constrain creativity as examples of learning community models and curriculum illustrate. At Fayetteville Technical Community College, for instance, faculty who are leading a new learning community initiative targeted courses with poor retention and high failure rates: Introductory Algebra and Basic Chemistry I and II. They began by designing an integrated module that addressed content in each course where students struggled most, followed this positive experience by designing more modules, and eventually created a team-taught integrated course.[13]

Examining different learning community approaches

Many learning community models envisioned in developmental education share a common goal: to increase students' achievement level. Like other learning communities models, those designed for developmental students are variations on three general types of learning community structures:[14]

a) *Interest group or "colloquy" model:* A small cohort of students enrolls in a set of two or three larger, unmodified and coherent set of classes (organized around a major, a topical inquiry, or interdisciplinary theme) and an integrative seminar that only the cohort attends. The seminar is the site for building community and curricular connections. The teaching team for the seminar varies (regular or adjunct faculty member, librarian, student affairs professional, peer mentor, graduate TA, or an instructional team of these colleagues).

b) *Paired or clustered classes:* Students co-register in two or more courses linked thematically or by content. Faculty members (and staff) coordinate syllabi and assignments, and work intentionally to build community and foster connections. Often courses are scheduled back-to-back to make a coherent time schedule and to "free space" for collaborative work, the end of one class and beginning of another a time when all teaching team members can be present for seminars, project work, and group presentations.

c) *Team-taught model:* Students enroll in a co-planned and co-taught program of study across disciplines and skill areas that is usually focused on a theme or question. Teaching teams of faculty members sometimes include student affairs professionals, counselors, and librarians. The blurring of boundaries

While many learning communities initially form based solely on the interests of two or more faculty rather than areas of student need, learning communities for students who are already at risk in higher education need to be located in curricular trouble spots.

The Pedagogy of Possibilities: Developmental Education, College-Level Studies, and Learning Communities between disciplines and courses favor a larger whole. This intense working together—and then working with students—represents faculty development at its best, highly-contextualized and particular, not generic; our learning is no different than our students' learning.

Some campus learning communities' initiatives include a variety of models along with linked assignments.

Investigating possibilities for integration

For some campus teams, the choice of learning community models depends on the common ground arrived at during a curricular planning workshop (Malnarich and Lardner 2003). An abilities-based approach that asks potential teaching partners the question used by Alverno to design its abilities-based curriculum is one way to discover common ground: What do we want students to know and be able to do as a result of their participation in a particular course? People individually reflect on what they value most in relation to student learning, what their aspirations are for their students, and the abilities, skills, ideas, habits of mind, and attitudes that represent specific course outcomes. The "teaching partners" share their work to discover potential areas for curricular integration. Agreement on common expectations or learning outcomes is a fertile ground for designing an integrative or "linked assignment" where two sets of students, from two different courses, work together on the same assignment or project that has been developed by "teaching partners." Often this exercise in creating a linked assignment leads to the assignment being implemented, and further experimentation. Some campus learning communities' initiatives include a variety of models along with linked assignments. This approach connects people who would like to become involved in learning communities but who also want to assess the impact on their students' learning before proceeding with a more integrated model.

Choosing models based on aims and circumstances

One clear structural advantage of most learning community models over stand-alone courses is that faculty and academic support staff have *more time, more space, and more resources* immediately at hand to work with new and underprepared students. As the case studies in Section Two indicate campus learning communities for developmental students are variations on the three general models. A data-driven analysis of student needs, collaborative possibilities from curriculum planning sessions, and available institutional resources (including staffing, scheduling, administrative support, and funding) are some of the factors underlying the mix of models a campus chooses to implement. Most campuses begin learning community work by linking courses together and scheduling them back-to-back. Some of these links are taught separately; some are fully integrated and team taught; some teams elect to teach some classes together. Elaborate models are not necessarily the best way to support students who are struggling in high-risk courses: simple links or pairs can be scaled-up to serve most underprepared students who arrive at college as the Grossmont Community College case study illustrates. A version of the Critical Inquiry seminar/course at Indiana University-Purdue University Indianapolis may reach many more students at large institutions than a coordinated studies program.

The following table groups different learning community programs briefly highlighted in the rest of this chapter in relation to effective curricular practices in developmental education.

Developmental education best practices and learning community (LC) examples

- *Adopt an abilities-based developmental perspective in LCs and throughout the campus*
  *California State University, Hayward–cluster with ability-based English component
  De Anza College–one lecture class/three different writing cohorts
  Sandhills Community College–flexible movement between developmental levels
  Seattle Central Community College–integrated program/range of abilities-based credits
  *Indiana University-Purdue University Indianapolis (IUPUI)–integrative seminar focused on developing all students' academic abilities

- *Target high-risk courses*
  Edmonds Community College-chemistry/math
  Fayetteville Technical and Community College-math/chemistry
  *Grossmont Community College-reading/writing links
  *Indiana University-Purdue University Indianapolis (IUPUI)–integrative seminar linked to electives, gateway courses
  Shoreline Community College-reading/writing/critical thinking three-course sequence
  *University of Texas at El Paso-math and pre-engineering/science cluster

- *Integrate skill development with college level courses (college credit)*
  De Anza College–developmental reading/writing pair linked with college courses
  Fayetteville Technical Community College–developmental writing/sociology
  LaGuardia Community College–developmental reading/writing/college level courses
  Northwest Indian College-TENRM–developmental first quarter in 2-year program
  Spokane Falls Community College–reading/study skills paired with multiple courses

- *Design a holistic program (integrate academic and student support services; use peer tutors)*
  Baltimore City College–student success/developmental course pair
  *California State University, Hayward–cluster includes academic success component
  *IUPUI–counselors
  UTEP science/engineering graduates) are advisors, mentors
  LaGuardia Community College–developmental reading/writing/speech cluster/counselor taught seminar

*scaled-up models

The Pedagogy of Possibilities: Developmental Education,
College-Level Studies, and Learning Communities

Including essential components in developmental learning communities

Learning communities for developmental students should be engaging, supportive, and challenging. Effective programs combine support with high expectations and intellectual rigor; they integrate skills and content, and are reading/writing intensive. Mathematics and science are also integral to these learning community efforts. Some learning communities that integrate developmental courses and college-level courses allow developmental students to earn college credit.

Our expectations regarding the quality of learning communities are not different for underprepared students. We recognize in John Tagg's account of an "awakening class," the kind of student and faculty engagement that is central to learning community work whether students are beginning, developing, or advanced in their studies:

> If a class goes well, there is a certain point in the term where it awakens, grows up, takes charge of itself, becomes a class instead of a group of strangers yoked unwillingly together . . . A class that is working is never really like any other because it really is negotiating its own meanings, negotiating itself . . . I can't define it, but I know it when I see it . . . When students come into the room, you can see that they know where they are, that it is no longer a strange place. This coming together as a new thing seems to me to happen sooner in learning communities. And I think that it happens more strongly too. (Tagg 2003, 262)

A community like this, though, does not develop by chance; a particular pedagogy makes it possible for students in Tagg's class to "take charge" of their learning in the way he describes. For instance, in *Teaching with Your Mouth Shut* (2000), the late Don Finkel, a masterful designer of conceptual workshops, describes a practice where the posing of an initial puzzle or contradiction hooks students into increasingly complex and reflective inquiry. They read a series of texts that illuminate aspects of the puzzle that they discuss with others, guided by questions and writing exercises.

Learning communities for developmental students may differ from other learning communities in one critical respect: we need to address students' approaches to learning explicitly. As the first monograph chapter "Taking the Risk to Learn" indicates, students need to explore their conceptions of learning and intelligence using a similar approach to the one Finkel describes. Challenging curriculum—especially focused on the theme of learning that examines research findings on learning and intelligence, learning theory, and related instructional and curriculum practices—supports students in a deep and enduring way by giving them the means to critique their school experience from a new position, that of an able learner.

Faculty experienced in creating collaborative learning environments take care to involve students in establishing the guidelines or social contract for creating a risk-taking community where everyone treats everyone's contributions with respect. By reframing risk taking as a collaborative practice not solely as an individual behavior, we offer less confident learners possibilities for peer-supported risk taking.

Effective programs combine support with high expectations and intellectual rigor; they integrate skills and content, and are reading/writing intensive.

Developing campus partnership and support

Learning communities for developmental students require campus-wide commitment and support that is problem-oriented and emphasizes collaborative problem solving. Data-based decisions on where to locate learning communities to benefit underprepared and struggling students require the cooperation of institutional research and the registrar's office. Bringing people together to coordinate their work with underprepared students—advising, counseling, tutoring, lab work, and classroom instruction in both developmental education and college-level courses—requires administrative support from different sectors of the academy. These steps that occur in the "fact-finding" planning phases of a developmental education learning community initiative do not incur additional financial costs but they require a campus commitment to *all* students' academic success. For many campuses, the problems associated with underprepared students have been left to developmental education, an area typically marginalized in the academy. "At risk" students are labeled as such because higher education institutions are still underdeveloped and poorly prepared to serve underrepresented students well; the "barriers to readiness" can be read as clues signaling practices that need to be rethought.

Learning communities give students, faculty, advisors, and counselors opportunities to know one another better so that they can collectively address institutional barriers to learning. For faculty who do not usually know who among their students are most "at risk" in higher education, the realization that people's ordinary lives means they probably will *not* graduate, even if they are good students, comes as a stunning surprise. People working in academic support and student affairs are far more knowledgeable about students' lives. At their best, learning communities bring these two sides of the academy together in a teaching team or support team. Maxwell (1979) views this intentional connection as a cornerstone of effective programs for underprepared students.

Once a campus begins to pool what is known about its underprepared students and what needs to be put in place so they can be supported in their studies, most learning communities for developmental students find ways to include counselors and advisors in the teaching team. Broader issues, including institutional policies are re-invented to better serve students who are "at risk" in higher education.

a) *At Baltimore City College (BCC)*, student affairs counselors and Skip Downing, the author of *On Course* (2002), a book about learning how to be responsible for your own learning at college used in many developmental classes, designed a learning community for developmental students that addressed issues related to "taking the risk to learn." Initiated in 1998, the learning community paired a developmental course in reading, writing, or mathematics with a student success class. The counselors who taught the student success part of the class conducted interviews with each student to better understand what barriers placed them at risk and what helped them succeed. The learning community became a place where students could talk and write about becoming successful: How can we get what we want? What are the strategies for getting there? Students became deeply committed to one

Learning communities for developmental students require campus-wide commitment and support that is problem-oriented and emphasizes collaborative problem solving.

another's successes. In the second semester, students moved to the next developmental course level and continued to meet with their mentors from the first semester. BCC tracked students for three semesters to Freshman Composition. Compared to their peers, these developmental learning community students' pass rate on the English exit exam was 78 percent on their first try compared to a pass rate of 50 percent for other students. Developmental students who passed at the higher rate were also enrolled in Freshmen Composition for the first time while many of their peers in the lower pass rate group were taking the class for the second, third, and fourth time. Math retention impressed faculty, but the success rate was not as dramatic.

b) *At Northwest Indian College*, the teaching team of the Tribal Environmental and Natural Resource Management (TENRM) Program realized that they needed to make two critical changes to their six-quarter learning community to better support students, including a change in college policy, after assessing the program's pilot year. First, they decided to redesign the first quarter to include an emphasis on developmental education and the mastery of basic scientific concepts and environmental sciences terminology. Second, they adopted a non-abandonment philosophy and policy in response to students' attendance. Northwest Indian College would calculate TENRM students' grade point average based on courses completed not courses attempted, and returning students would be welcomed back and given assistance to complete missed work. The program's external evaluator, Joan LaFrance, credits high completion rates to the close ties developed between faculty and students in the learning community that helped the faculty team from Huxley College of the Environment at Western Washington University and NWIC's science and mathematics division understand the reality of most Indian and Alaskan Native students' lives. Staying in college is extraordinarily difficult for students who may have to be absent for an extended period owing to personal circumstances, family responsibilities, and cultural traditions. (See Section Two for more information on the Lummi Nation tribal college's learning community.)

c) *At LaGuardia Community College (CUNY)* in New York, students speak more than 100 different languages. The learning communities program that began in 1976 with liberal arts clusters initiated a New Student House (NSH) for developmental students in 1991-92, followed three years later by a New Student ESL House. Very poor retention rates for developmental students led to the creation of the learning cluster for developmental students. A counselor teaches the Freshman Seminars in the NSHs and, in the case of developmental students, faculty regularly meet with the counselor who offers guidance on students who are most at risk in the program. Many two- and four-year institutions from across the country have adapted both NSH models. Each New House cluster includes a three-credit college class and a one-credit Freshman Seminar. (See Section Two for a more detailed account of this program).

Staying in college is extraordinarily difficult for students who may have to be absent for an extended period owing to personal circumstances, family responsibilities, and cultural traditions.

Working at appropriate developmental levels

Some of the most successful learning community models remove barriers to learning that developmental educators create for students through a rigid adherence to sequenced developmental courses based on placement assessments. At Greenville Technical College in South Carolina, students' grade levels went up one course level after people attended review workshops before taking Compass and Asset entry assessments,[15] a finding that suggests that an over-reliance on this kind of assessment would be unwise. Many learning communities prefer to adopt a flexible and abilities-based approach to placing students and awarding credit.

a) *At Seattle Central Community College* (SCCC),[16] coordinated studies programs developed in the mid-1980s integrated ESL, developmental writing and reading courses, and English composition with content drawn from two or more introductory college-level courses. This learning community structure that is continually being refined allows students to "move" to appropriate writing levels despite placement results. A recognized leader in learning communities, SCCC awards credit for the highest writing level reached based on the quality of students' written work. This approach encourages students to focus on writing as a means for effective communication. For more information contact Audrey Wright, awrigh@sccd.ctc.edu.

b) *At De Anza Community College,* in Cupertino, California, faculty from different departments created a new learning community model. In their learning communities' program, they encourage students whose abilities as writers *differ widely* to enroll in a large college-level lecture course. They then regroup students into three distinct composition cohort links: English as a Second Language, Developmental English, and College English. Using material from the lecture courses, these writing classes offer obvious support to students, but something of greater value: the message that they can do college level work. (See Section Two of monograph).

c) *At Sandhills Community College* in Pinehurst, North Carolina, more than 60 percent of entering students do not meet college entrance requirements in mathematics, writing, or reading, while over 50 percent need developmental work in more than one area. Integrated by theme, Sandhills' learning communities include developmental and college-level courses. Students can earn college credit and advance into the next developmental course level any time based on their work. For more information, contact Alfreda Stroman, stromana@sandhills.edu.

High expectations and intellectual rigor

The Schillings studied the "expectations gap" between student expectations and faculty expectations at several colleges and universities. The research findings confirmed the wide distance between faculty and students: faculty expect students to spend three times the amount of time on their studies than they expect to spend. After one year in higher education, though, they actually spend less time than their original estimate. As to "deep learning," students read more textbooks than primary sources, memorize formulas in science rather than applying the scientific method, and use passive studying strategies rather than those associated with higher order thinking skills. Finally, the patterns of time use students establish in the first year of their studies are repeated throughout their undergraduate experience.

Developmental students' experience at college begins when they arrive. The Schillings' research suggests that for these students to do well in subsequent years, they need to be challenged, a point made by Clifford Adelman in his research and discussed in Chapter Two. The view that challenging curriculum undermines students' confidence and chances to be successful could not be further from the truth.

The Schillings report that campus participants in the expectations study came to think about the problem as "students being on the job without a job description" (Schilling and Schilling 1999, 9). In brief, faculty do not translate high expectations *into practice*. This does not refer to harder grading but to "heightening the intellectual challenge of courses, moving beyond memorization to engaged critical analysis that creates excitement for students. Our work suggests that it is crucial to do this in the very first semester of college, or students will resist any attempts to raise the stakes in the later years in college" (10).

One of the campuses involved in the study, a major research and open-admissions university, chose to *raise* its expectations for all students. The campus student profile is similar to that of commuter community colleges: 60 percent of beginning students are first-generation college students, 75 percent do not meet college-level reading, writing or mathematics placement requirements, and nearly half of the student body are enrolled part time.

At Indiana University-Purdue University Indianapolis (IUPUI), the decision to expect more of most students led to the creation of Critical Inquiry (CI), a one-to-two-credit-hour course where students are introduced to the expectations and requirements for successful college learning. The CI Handbook for faculty and staff participants notes that the CI program is "open to all, but strongly recommended for first- and second-year students."[17] The university, determined to avoid the stigma attached to developmental education, purposefully provides transitional support for *all* students through the CI seminars that are linked to an introductory discipline-based course or a course in area studies such as Afro-American Studies, Women's Studies, or Communication Studies. The seminar meets twice a week for two and one-half hours of instruction time. Materials and assignments are coordinated with discipline faculty who are closely involved in seminar curricular design and implementation. The CI model also connects students to electives, gateway courses, and a required freshman composition course. While each CI is distinctive, they also share consistent learning outcomes, seminar requirements, and an expectation-setting contract, "A Partnership for Academic Excellence," signed by each student. Unlike most freshmen seminars, CI is resource-intensive, team planned and executed. The planning and teaching team includes a faculty member, a librarian and technology expert, an advisor, and a peer mentor. CIs are introduced at orientation to entering students and their families, and discussed at advising sessions; they are also recommended as one option to fulfill second semester academic support requirements for conditionally admitted freshmen. For further information, contact Barbara Jackson, bjackson@iupui.edu.

Integrating skills and content

As Chapter Two indicates, when skill and content teaching are integrated, struggling students do better in their studies. Developmental educators reached this conclusion in the 1920s, again in the 1970s, and repeated the finding several times more in field-based best practice summaries published in the last ten years. Effective developmental courses use college curriculum to develop students' basic academic abilities, not an array of generic skills. One clear benefit of integrating skill and content courses is that developmental educators, over time, will be able to identify the academic language that students need to master to be effective learners in higher education. For instance, an examination of introductory textbooks for the disciplines suggests some of this common vocabulary (and understanding). Words used without explanation include model, theory, perspective, paradigm, principle, policy, formula, argument, concept, fact, and so on.

At Spokane Falls Community College (SFCC), one popular model in the learning communities' program integrates a reading and/or study skills strategy course with a content course from liberal arts or a platform course in professional and technical programs that is offered as a linked course. In 2003, for example, study skills and reading were linked with Introductory Chemistry and English Composition. Content specialists incorporate study strategies and skills into their broader teaching practice, and reading and study skills specialists develop a content-specific understanding of the learning challenges students face in an entry-level college course. (See Section Two for an account of SFCC's developmental learning communities.)

Reading and writing intensive developmental programs

Students can know they belong in college by doing "real" college-level work. Unlike many skill-based developmental reading courses where students actually do very little reading and, as a consequence, programs have been judged as woefully ineffective (Adelman 1999; Maxwell 1998), the following examples of developmental learning communities are reading and writing intensive.

a) *At Shoreline Community College*, a three-course Developmental English sequence integrates reading, writing, thinking, and learning skills.[18] Faculty expect students to develop these abilities by reading intellectually stimulating texts that would be assigned to any entering student and by composing essays in all levels of developmental writing. The program's cornerstone is an eleven-part reading process that students eventually internalize and master. Students develop questions for further inquiry, identify the issues they want to pursue through study and discussion with others, and construct

One clear benefit of integrating skill and content courses is that developmental educators, over time, will be able to identify the academic language that students need to master to be effective learners in higher education.

their own "vocabulary list" of key terms and background knowledge they need to understand to fully grasp authors' intended meanings. (See Section Two.)

b) *At Grossmont Community College*, Project Success exemplifies how a small, doable practice such as creating a developmental reading and developmental writing link can be scaled up from one course to many that meet the needs of hundreds of students each term. The faculty teams who teach in these developmental links know the power of an engaging book and they take time to discuss the merits of different proposed books. Project Success is an inspiring example of a modest educational reform that began in developmental education, spread to the disciplines, and is now involving programs for honor students. Project Success also uses a simple and very effective mentoring method for introducing new faculty to the philosophy and practice of learning communities. (See Section Two.)

The faculty teams who teach in these developmental links know the power of an engaging book and they take time to discuss the merits of different proposed books.

Mathematics and science for developmental students

A study by the Institute for Research in Higher Education found that 57 percent of developmental students who learned mathematics over a fifteen-to-twenty-year period had been exposed to at least two or more radical changes in curriculum and pedagogy, an insight into why so many students may find mathematics confusing and/or why some students have gaps in their understanding of basic mathematical conceptions (Duranczyk and Caniglia 1998). Mathematics classes that include writing assignments encourage students to reason their way through problems, and learning communities that adopt this strategy help students deepen their understanding of mathematics; other learning communities integrate mathematics with science, a combination that helps students understand how math is used in the world. "Bridge" learning communities that provide an orientation for first-year students often offer refresher workshops in mathematics so students who typically do not use the mathematics they have learned can brush up on specific math skills without having to redo a basic course.

a) *At Edmonds Community College*, one of the first community colleges campuses to offer learning communities in math/science in the nation, CheMath, links developmental math with a pre-college level chemistry course. This developmental math/science learning community has served as a model for learning communities at a number of other community colleges around the country. In a study of 539 students in college-level Chemistry, 139 were considered to be at risk based on placement scores. In this at risk population, the 62 students who had taken the CheMath learning community, who had lower placement scores than the other 77 students, still fared better: their completion rates and average GPA were higher. For more information, contact Mary O'Brien, mobrien@edcc.edu.

b) *At the University of Texas at El Paso* (UTEP), a minority-serving institution, many students are first-generation who would be considered "at risk" in higher education. The CircLES (Circle of Learning for Entering Students) program, a learning communities cluster for entering full-time science and engineering students, begins with a weeklong summer orientation with opportunities to review math skills before writing a placement assessment. In their first two semesters at UTEP, students in the CircLES program take a mathematics course, an English course, a Seminar in Critical Inquiry, and a discipline-specific course. Counselors, who are UTEP graduates from science and engineering, provide academic advising, scheduling, and career planning and mentoring. (See Section Two.)

Earning college level credit

Earning college credit and developing academic skills for entrance requirements and college-level courses at the same time is an extraordinary motivator, as Patricia Cross pointed out in *Beyond the Open Door*. That students do so, not as marginalized members of the academic community but as fully entitled members, is a hallmark of both some well-known and successful learning community programs and some programs in the early stages of development.

a) *At De Anza College,* the *Learning in Communities (LinC) Program* includes links, clusters, and cohorts which combine developmental classes with general education courses: "[we assume] that students who place in developmental classes are quite capable of successfully completing course work in a general education class at the same time" (Stoll 1999, 17). In fall 1998, when De Anza first experimented with linking classes in developmental and general education, it instituted a carefully documented assessment process. In the pilot developmental reading, writing, and speech communications cluster, *Experiences and Expressions*, 100 percent of the students completed the class, 89 percent continued their studies in the next quarter, 100 percent who took the college-level writing assessment passed, and 92 percent of the students received a "C" or better in all three classes. Collaboration between the LinC Program and an in-house staff development program ensures that the quality of learning community work continues as the program expands. Ongoing assessment is at the heart of the LinC program's success. (See Section Two.)

b) *At California State University, Hayward*, the General Education First Year Cluster Program invites all entering students—including freshmen whose results from statewide mandatory English and mathematics proficiency tests identify them as "remedial students"—to choose among a number of theme-based learning community clusters for their first year of undergraduate studies. Cal State Hayward made a conscious decision not to create isolated cohorts for developmental students. Instead, the cluster coursework for each quarter includes several components that all students take, among these a discipline-based course linked to an information literacy class, speech, and an academic success component. Only an English component offers composition classes at different developmental levels (math is offered separately from the learning community clusters). Developmental students enroll in and complete college-level, discipline-based coursework as successfully as students who are not required to take developmental writing courses. Even though more than 55 percent of entering students enroll in a developmental-level writing course—and some place in the lowest level requiring them to take a three-quarter sequence—most freshmen complete the general education composition course in their first year. (See Section Two.)

c) *At Parkland College* in Champaign, Illinois, entering students who place at seventh-to-ninth-grade reading levels or tenth-to-twelfth-grade reading levels are enrolled in two distinct *Integrated Studies Communities* (ISC). Both include a college-level transfer course that would ordinarily not be available to students who did not meet college-level reading requirements. Students that place in the lower reading courses take ISC II, which includes developmental reading and writing, an orientation to college course, and introductory speech. Students in the next level of developmental reading take ISC III that includes writing and psychology. These team-taught learning communities involve extensive coordination and integration. The success experienced by students in these ISCs since they were established in 1998 led Parkland to develop learning communities across disciplines and for students in honors programs. For more information, contact Jody Littleton, jlittleton@parkland.edu.

d) *At Skagit Valley Community College*, in Mount Vernon, Washington, students must successfully complete three interdisciplinary learning community combinations to meet transfer degree requirements, and learning communities for developmental students are recognized as one option. Some choices include: "The Reading-Writing Connection," developmental reading and writing; "What's the problem?", developmental math and writing; and, "*En Otros Terminos*/In Other Words," Spanish 101 and English Grammar. For more information, contact Lynn Dunlap, dunlap@skagit.ctc.edu.

e) *At Bethune-Cookman College*, in Daytona Beach, Florida, an Historically Black College and University (HBCU) that is focusing its learning community efforts on first-year students, one learning community, "From Africa to the Americas," gives entering developmental students a jumpstart in achieving college credits. The program includes a freshman seminar, African American history, freshman English, and reading classes. For more information go to www.bethune.cookman.edu.

Assessing the impact of learning communities and collaborative learning
Vincent Tinto and his graduate students Anne Goodsell-Love and Pat Russo in 1994 did the first major study of the impact of learning communities as part of a five-year longitudinal research project on student learning in higher education

conducted by the National Center on Postsecondary Teaching, Learning, and Assessment. A broad definition of student learning was used: the learning of basic knowledge in science, mathematics, and the social sciences; cognitive abilities, such as oral and written communication skills, critical thinking, and problem solving; the development of students' values and attitudes toward learning; and progress, persistence, performance, and degree attainment (Ratcliff and Associates 1995, 4).

The Collaborative Learning Project examined the academic and social experiences of beginning students in three learning community programs: the Freshman Interest Group (FIG) program at the University of Washington, the Coordinated Studies Program (CSP) at Seattle Central Community College, and the learning community clusters at LaGuardia Community College in New York. The research team sought answers to these questions: do collaborative learning programs make a difference in student learning and persistence? And, if so, how? The institutions selected for this study faced two different but common problems that affect student engagement: size in the case of the large residential university and time in the cases of the two urban community colleges. In fact, on many two-year campuses nearly two-thirds of the student body work part time and almost one-quarter are student commuters spending anywhere from six to twenty hours a week traveling to and from class (CCSSE 2002).

The researchers identified four key findings. First, a community of peers encourages class participation and continued attendance, and groups formed in class often continue to meet outside class, to socialize and to study. Second, collaborative pedagogy through team teaching and classroom activities adds an intellectual diversity and richness that encourages students' own intellectual development and participation as one of many voices. Third, students' academic performance and persistence increase in collaborative learning settings. Finally, collaborative learning works for commuter students and for students in big impersonal places (Tinto et al. 1993, 20-21). This study on collaborative learning broke new ground not because it ties student involvement to student attainment but because, as the researchers note

> . . . it moves our conversation . . . to the practical issue of how involvement can be generated in settings where it is not easily obtained. Our research also suggests that we need to give serious attention to the argument that the attainment of the goals of enhanced student involvement and achievement is possible only when institutions alter the settings in which students are asked to learn. (21)

Learning communities were an effective way of altering the settings even in commuter schools. Others researchers would make similar observations. For instance, Grubb and associates, in a later study of learning communities in community colleges, note: "students report that they come to know their fellow students better and are able to work with them more both in and out of class—in contrast to conventional practice in community colleges, where students typically find a new group virtually every class they take" (1999, 264). A recent National Learning Communities Project monograph, *Learning Community Research and*

Our research also suggests that we need to give serious attention to the argument that the attainment of the goals of enhanced student involvement and achievement is possible only when institutions alter the settings in which students are asked to learn.

Assessment: What We Know Now, examined over 150 learning community assessment reports and research studies, and concludes that learning communities unequivocally enhance retention, persistence, student satisfaction, and achievement (Taylor, et al. 2003).

Almost a decade after the results of the Collaborative Learning Project became known, the *Engaging Community Colleges* (CCSSE 2002) report revealed that among the 33,500 students surveyed 15 percent of part-time and 7 percent of full-time students never worked on projects during class with their classmates. Forty-five percent of part-time and 29 percent of full-time students never worked to prepare assignments outside class, and 51 percent of part-time and 39 percent of full-time students "never discussed ideas from readings or classes with an instructor outside class" (6-9). This quantified account of student disengagement speaks to what Hill refers to as the isolation of the modern college and why learning communities need to become a mainstream practice in higher education. The companion study, the 2002 National Survey of Student Engagement indicated that involvement in learning communities was positively associated with gains on all five benchmarks of educational practice: level of academic challenge; active and collaborative learning; student interactions with faculty members; supportive campus environment; and enriching educational experience.

Friendship through scholarship

In the Tinto and associates study, a student in the University of Washington's FIG program describes her experience in this way: "We were all learning together, but each person learns differently . . . I mean studying for tests and stuff. We helped each other . . . copying notes days we missed, dividing things up. I know that this girl and I did that a lot. Just studying for things and talking to each other about our projects" (Tinto et al. 1993, 18). In the same study a student in Seattle Central Community College's coordinated studies program says this about her experience: "These classes incorporate into your life and into your learning. It becomes part of your thinking. It just keeps connecting, and connecting, and connecting" (19). Even students whose experience in learning communities is minimal, identify the same things in-depth research studies cite as key reasons for why learning communities work.

The language of the student quoted from the Pasadena TLC.XL program is revealing: "If you work hard, ask for help, support each other, then we'll all make it." Value is placed on the reciprocity associated with peer support, the means for "making it." Most of the summer bridge students still go to the Teaching and Learning Center every day to work on their assignments in small groups or teams. On the other side of the country, a number of Fayetteville Technical Community College students credit ongoing peer support as the reason they are still in school. They, too, continue to meet although their learning community course is over. One student in that semester's chemistry and math link offered to help students in her English class with their writing on her own time, using the learning community's "give a helping hand up" model. These two groups of students, enrolled in developmental classes at commuter colleges,

These classes incorporate into your life and into your learning. It becomes part of your thinking. It just keeps connecting, and connecting, and connecting"

believe they do their best work when they collaborate. Independent of faculty, they adapt the collaborative practices from their first learning community experience to other academic contexts. In both places, a network of mini-study groups is part of their student culture.

Vincent Tinto in an *AAHE Bulletin* article "Learning Communities, Collaborative Learning, and the Pedagogy of Educational Citizenship" uses the expression "learning the disposition of citizenship" (1995, 11) to describe unexpected research findings. He is surprised that students are learning citizenship through the practice of collaborative learning. Speaking of Seattle Central Community College students in particular, he notes that they "expressed a deepened appreciation for the importance of inclusive, supportive community in their lives. And they seemed to have awakened to the important notion that their own educational well-being was dependent on that of other members of the learning community, and it was in their own educational interest to be concerned with the educational needs of others" (12).

Tinto's comment about learning the disposition of citizenship reminds us that the educational project—the one Freire speaks of where "knowledge emerges only through invention and re-invention, through the restless, impatient, continuing, hopeful inquiry human beings pursue in the world, with the world, and each other" —is the gift access gives us. It is the promise of an embracing, yet messy, democracy.

Endnotes

1. This account of learning communities is drawn from National Learning Communities Project materials developed by Washington Center staff.

2. See Smith, et al. (forthcoming), or see http://learningcommons.evergreen.edu for a detailed summary of each model.

3. The phrase "friendship through scholarship" was used at a Washington State Learning Community Coordinators October 2003 meeting to describe what works for students in learning communities.

4. For more information about De Anza's program, see www.deanza.fhda.edu/linc/.

5. Other pedagogies include the intentional fostering of community, attending to diversity, connected knowing, linking theory to practice, and reflective practice and synthesis.

6. Before coming to Evergreen, Hill, while a professor of philosophy at the State University of New York, Stony Brook, invented federated learning communities (FLC), a model which "federates" three courses around an overarching theme and an integrating seminar led by a "master learner." This model learner, a faculty member from a discipline outside those represented in the FLC, attends all classes, does the work assigned, and helps students discover connections and contentions across the curriculum.

7. See the monograph on learning communities and diversity by Lardner (forthcoming) for an in-depth account of students' experience.

8. Kenneth Bruffee (1986) describes the knowledge the group constructs as "a consensus arrived at for the time being by communities of knowledgeable peers" (777) in a bibliographic essay on the social construction of knowledge

beginning with Thomas Kuhn's *Structure of Scientific Revolutions* and including *Local Knowledge*, the work of anthropologist Clifford Geertz.

9. Cited in van Slyck (1997, 152); see Pratt (1991, 34).

10. See Smith, et al. (forthcoming) for an account of the origins of learning community work.

11. See National Council on Education in the Disciplines (2001), *Mathematics and Democracy: The Case for Quantitative Literacy*.

12. Freshman Interest Groups or FIGs are found at many research universities because the model creates oases of small academic communities in large impersonal institutional settings. Typically three courses are offered around an interdisciplinary topic or course related to a major. Each FIG is convened by a more advanced student who acts as a peer advisor. The group meets weekly to study, learn more about campus resources, and plan co-curricular activities.

13. See Section Two for a longer account of this program.

14. See http://learningcommons.evergreen.edu for a more detailed account of learning community models/diagrams.

15. After six hours of college success skills workshops—two hours of basic skills instruction in reading, mathematics, and writing plus test-taking tips— 59 percent of the students improved their writing scores with 37 percent testing out of developmental writing. Sixty-seven percent improved their reading scores with 57 percent testing out of developmental reading, and 39 percent improved their mathematics scores with 7 percent testing out of developmental mathematics (Grastie 1998, 60-61).

16. Developmental educators have named SCCC's learning community program as a best practice developmental education program (McCabe 2003).

17. From the University College U112, Critical Inquiry Handbook (2003,1) available from Barbara Jackson, bjackson@iupui.edu.

18. Entering students, initially assessed as the least able readers and writers, pass freshman composition at three times the Washington state average—60 percent compared to 21 percent. Also, students who complete their developmental program graduate at higher rates than the college average.

A Call for Action

The Parity of Esteem:
Students' Aspirations and Our Work as Educators

We respect developmental education because of its risk taking, its fundamental value system, and its expressed commitment to an academic underclass, those students who are frequently ignored, shoved to the side, and mistreated on many campuses . . . I am particularly concerned that the mounting attacks against developmental education are based on intolerance, racism, misunderstanding, ignorance, prejudice, and selfishness. I have not devoted 30-plus years of my life to higher education to want to see the clock set back.

John N. Gardner, Preface, *Developmental Education: Preparing Successful College Students*, (Higbee and Dwinell)

In October 1999 the General College of the University of Minnesota and its Center for Research on Developmental Education and Urban Literacy convened the First Intentional Meeting on Future Directions in Developmental Education. Twenty-one local, regional, and national leaders from the developmental education field met for two days of intense discussion. People whose scholarship has been cited in this monograph—Martha Maxwell, Hunter Boylan, David Arendale, and Martha Casazza—joined other teachers, researchers, economists, and administrators. In the foreword to the meeting's published proceedings, Terence Collins and David Taylor alert us to why we should be concerned: ". . . policy makers and legislators are in *full retreat* from the principle of broad access" (2000, 5; emphasis added).

Before turning to the conclusions reached by participants, we look briefly at state policies related to developmental education followed by an account of a February day that crystallizes for me, at least, what is at stake and what this implies for the work of educators.

Undermining education's purpose and possibilities

Since John Gardner declared his unequivocal support for developmental education, the situation has deteriorated. Findings from a fall 2001 survey conducted by the Center for Community Policy at the Education Commission of the States (ECS) confirm a disturbing trend. In ten states, public four-year institutions are discouraged or prohibited from offering "remedial education": Arizona, Colorado, Georgia, Florida, Indiana, Kansas, New Mexico, South Carolina, Utah, and Virginia. By 2005, all of Louisiana's four-year institutions will not be allowed to enroll students who need developmental classes. The City University of New York (CUNY) is phasing out developmental education at four-year institutions, a stance now adopted by the California State University system. In Massachusetts, no more than 10 percent of the students enrolled can receive developmental instruction.

Earlier we noted that 41 percent of first time students in *all* undergraduate institutions currently take at least one developmental course in reading, writing, or mathematics. In the ECS study, twenty-nine states were able to estimate the percentage of entering students in fall 2001 that would need developmental education. Among four-year institutions, eight states place the figure at 25 percent or higher, with Connecticut the lowest at 5.5 percent and Indiana the highest at 50 percent (ECS 2002, 4). By comparison, among two-year colleges, eighteen states place the figure of entering students needing developmental education at 40 percent or higher, with Alabama lowest at 10.4 percent and Tennessee highest at 70.9 percent. Among the forty-seven states responding to the ECS survey, a dozen or more states are debating the following policy issues: whether to limit or eliminate remedial courses in higher education; whether to make community colleges solely responsible for remedial education; and whether to charge K-12 systems for high school graduates who need remediation. Nine states are debating whether developmental education should be contracted out. Four states—Alaska, Nebraska, Wisconsin, and Wyoming—prohibit the use of state financial aid for developmental education.

Both four-year and two-year institutions in the country are already cutting back in tutoring, counseling, and advising that have been lifesavers for incoming students who require support as they adjust to a new academic culture and the challenges of demanding college work . . .

Many institutions dedicated in practice to the democratization of higher education find themselves in a precarious place where budget cutbacks leave little recourse but to raise tuition even though student aid budgets can barely keep up with escalating college and tuition costs. In its May 30, 2003, cover story the *Chronicle of Higher Education* compares budget cuts at three institutions in Washington state—the University of Washington-Seattle (UW-Seattle), Eastern Washington University (EWU), and Seattle Central Community College (SCCC)—to illustrate a trend that is repeated in other states. At first glance, budget cuts to community colleges that serve the neediest, most academically underprepared and economically disenfranchised appear to be lower than cuts to universities. The cuts, though, turn out to be disproportionately high for community colleges since they represent a greater percentage of an institution's total budget. If we map onto this picture students' race and ethnicity[1] and whether an institution is highly selective like UW-Seattle or open admissions like the other two institutions—combined with what we know about at-risk students and a family's economic status—rising tuition defers the dreams of the most underrepresented students in higher education. Both four-year and two-year institutions in the country are already cutting back in tutoring, counseling, and advising that have been lifesavers for incoming students who require support as they adjust to a new academic culture and the challenges of demanding college work (National Center for Public Policy and Higher Education 2002).

Rigid placement policies also threaten to undermine research-based best practices in developmental education, especially those related to integrated learning and learning community work. In twenty states, placement in developmental courses is determined at the state level by statute and/or board policy even though "degrees of preparedness" are highly contextual (Maxwell 1979). Florida, Georgia, North Carolina, South Dakota, Tennessee, Texas, and Wyoming have a state-mandated exam.[2] For educators working on integrated learning initiatives that straddle developmental- and college-level courses, the findings related to "concurrent enrollment" undercut educators' expertise and judgment: "In many states, students can take remedial courses in conjunction with occupational programs, but must complete remedial coursework before taking general education courses" (ECS 2002, 3). Among states responding to the survey, Maryland requires students to complete developmental coursework *before* taking college-level courses.

Radical policy changes at a state level are not matched by equally radical changes on other fronts requiring attention such as aligning "misaligned expectations" or reducing the effect of "risk factors" or closing the "academic achievement gap" that surfaces as early as elementary school and persists up to graduate studies (see Chapter 1). Nor have placement assessments been scrutinized in relation to what they do or do not reveal about students' abilities in reading, writing, and mathematics.

The full consequences of all of these policy decisions for students—and for campuses that struggle to serve them well—have not yet been tracked. But we know who will be immediately affected by regressive policies: at-risk students who work hard to realize high hopes. Many are minority, low-income, or disadvantaged students; some are recent immigrants and refugees; others are adults returning to school for job retraining. Where will people go who are turned away from public four-year institutions . . . then from public two-year institutions . . . and at what social cost? To date, higher education's collective voice has not been raised in support of people's right to an education and the role played by developmental education in the long trek toward an education of quality for all. Nor have we mounted an offensive against policies that derail years of work by educators less well known than John Gardner whose convictions about the purpose and benefits of an educated citizenry have transformed higher education for the better.

Choosing among contradictory realities

A day in February 2003 reminds me about the deep rifts in public education that countless people work so hard to repair, and why a practical commitment to access, equity, and a first-class education for all must be supported as a crucial public good. Faced with contradictory realities, we need to be intentional about the choices we make.

In the morning, I meet with an Evergreen internship student to discuss her work as a librarians' aid at an urban inner-city elementary school for poor and frequently homeless children. We look at a girl's writing that describes a video she likes along with my student's annotations of a paragraph the girl read during a tutoring session. What does she know how to do as a reader and as a writer? How might Vygotsky's idea of the zone of proximal development apply to working with her on reading and writing? Beyond the shock of how far below expected skill levels this sixth-grade youngster's work appears to be (yet entirely expected in keeping with her actual school attendance), we discover an inventive bright mind and internally coherent language use. The internship is difficult. Small advances are followed by long absences; children disappear. Classroom teachers insist that children sent to the library must complete drill exercises on basic skills before they can use the computers (their favorite activity) or read books and draw (my student's preferred activity with them). The family literacy program my student is working on is hard to organize when privation is constant, multiple languages are spoken, and the idea of a family learning how to use a public library together flounders on a simple rule—you need a home address to check out books.

In the afternoon, Washington Center co-hosts a meeting for developmental educators with the Washington State Board for Community and Technical Colleges at South Puget Sound Community College. During a first presentation, instructors and some administrators from mainly two-year institutions discuss findings from a telephone research study conducted in the summer of 2002 on current concerns in the field, how students are placed in courses, and innovative programs underway, including examples of integrated curriculum within developmental education and linked courses between developmental education, English as a Second Language, and college-level courses.[3] The researchers identified many common themes and concerns voiced by the majority of faculty and administrators. Among these, several stand out in relation to the monograph's intent to encourage greater collaboration across a campus in support of differently prepared students' learning. First, the people canvassed feel demoralized by the stigma their students and they experience; second, they report that communication with college-level instructors is strained and the two faculty groups do not work often or well together; third, they think students need to receive continued support since completing developmental classes is not necessarily the equivalent of college readiness; and fourth, they worry that the gap between developmental exit standards and college entry standards reinforces the idea among students that developmental courses are gatekeepers that waste students' time and prevent them from furthering their education. By contrast, faculty who teach linked or clustered courses describe their experience in very different ways. Most of the people interviewed do not know about Washington state's College Readiness Project.

The next presentation reintroduces the College Readiness project, completed a few years earlier, to a group of mainly new faculty, the majority who are adjuncts and part-timers. They want to know where they can find the original study, typical student assignments, and the rubric for student learning outcomes that, if mastered, would signal "readiness" for college-level work. A rumor that a state official is thinking of renaming developmental education prompts cynical comments. Some respondents to the summer questionnaire are in the room and "feeling stigmatized" is one of the main issues facing instructors and students; they doubt that a name change will neutralize an environment where they feel their work is increasingly marginalized and its value questioned.

In the evening, a sixth annual gala fund-raiser and banquet is underway at the same college that made its room available to us in the afternoon. The event is co-hosted by a group of African American and Native American parents and community members whose motto, "Education is the key to our future," connects their many activities. The founder, Larry Jenkins, kept asking kids who rode in his school bus what it would take for them to continue their education. Eventually they told him—money. Since 1997 the Thurston Group has organized its own Students of Color College Recruiting Weekend to help local minority high school students move on to higher education.[4] This evening is part of a bigger event, the Student Tour of Historically Black Colleges and Universities (HBCUs). Representatives from the different institutions in the South, where Thurston County students will visit, are here, along with some from Washington state's two- and four-year institutions.

President Suber from Saint Augustine's College, Raleigh, North Carolina, is speaking. She explains that her college, started by prominent Episcopal clergy in 1867, was established after the Civil War to educate freed African Americans. The mission has not really changed over time: "In the beginning potential, in the end results." These words, repeated several times during her speech, draw people together—parents of potential students, community supporters, and educators from elementary schools, community colleges, and universities. In the anecdotes she tells about different students whose lives have been changed at Saint Augustine's College, the message is clear: everyone can learn and our work as educators is to make sure motivated students realize their potential.

We are listening to the best version of ourselves as educators. In fact, the entire event is part of a long tradition where communities' grass roots organizing efforts secure the next generation's well-being through education. This tradition extends from outside the academy to within, where educators in the tradition of Saint Augustine's College "make a way" for the newly come. As Terence Collins writes:

> If we take a long view we see that developmental education traces its many roots to Reconstruction, to the Morill Land Grant Act, to the Progressive Era, to the Workers' Colleges of the Great Depression, to the G.I. Bill of Rights, to the Civil Rights Movement, to the Community College explosion of the late-mid-Twentieth Century, and to the Open Admissions movement that followed hard upon these latter events. We in developmental education are heirs to various movements of optimism about human possibility and the transformative possibilities of higher education. We and our students enact daily a peculiarly American optimism about human change and intellectual growth. (2002, v)

Despite the field's tenuous foothold within higher education, its essential contribution looks very different from outside the academy by people trying to get in. Developmental educators stand with other colleagues who are allies in the long protracted struggle for inclusion, social justice, and civil rights through the means of education. In the midst of contradictory realities, wise choices need to be made.

Naming the challenges ahead

From the outset of this monograph, we have been hopeful about our capacity as educators—whatever our area of expertise—to work collaboratively to solve the problems experienced by students new and underprepared for college. When representatives from the developmental education field met in October 1999 to discuss challenges and propose future directions "in the face of a full retreat from the principle of broad access" (Collins and Taylor 2000, 5), they did so with developmental education's historic legacy in mind as well as the immediate reality that the work undertaken by developmental education programs to support student learning, especially in four-year public institutions, would need to be reconfigured.

We in developmental education are heirs to various movements of optimism about human possibility and the transformative possibilities of higher education.

The times call for us to move to a new stage in learning community work—one from designing and supporting learning communities for a relatively small number of students to one that embraces the full potential of learning communities to serve many more students, especially those who are underrepresented in higher education.

Among the many issues and ideas named in the record of proceedings from this October meeting, the "challenge of mainstreaming developmental education" (7-9) is the most immediate and critical one to address. With waning support for developmental education, how can we embed the best practices into the core curriculum of undergraduate education? The circumstances require us to collectively challenge an elitist academic culture that deems certain kinds of learning less worthy than others, a call to action K. Patricia Cross made so long ago. Perhaps we can treat students who are struggling to learn something new in the way we would treat someone who is dear to us: we celebrate accomplishments and we offer consistent support.

The times call for us to move to a new stage in learning community work—one from designing and supporting learning communities for a relatively small number of students to one that embraces the full potential of learning communities to serve many more students, especially those who are underrepresented in higher education. To accomplish this aim, we invite educators involved in learning community work to intentionally seek out their developmental education colleagues—including those with little or no experience in learning communities—to advance our common work on several fronts.

a) *Learning communities need to be situated where students struggle most with their studies.* We need to use institutional data to help us shift from an emphasis on "boutique" offerings on the margins of campus practice to learning communities designed to improve all students' learning in both developmental education and college-level studies, carefully tracking the results for students most at-risk in higher education.

b) *Faculty and teaching teams need to base expectations for student learning on abilities-based criteria and standards, articulated within a developmental perspective.* We need to think through learning outcomes for beginning, developing, and advanced performance, so we can encourage and challenge students to go beyond their own expectations for learning.

c) *Campuses need to provide institutional support for research-based pedagogy and curriculum development.* We need to develop in-house educational opportunities for teams of educators to learn about current research-based best practices in developmental education and learning communities' work. We also need to reorganize our time so we can develop, implement, and assess plans designed to support students new and underprepared for college level studies.

This shift in emphasis from learning community offerings planned by faculty excited by the prospects of teaching together to scaled-up efforts requiring broad-based collaboration between developmental educators and learning community practitioners is daring, difficult work.

In truth, the day in February sharpened this monograph's purpose. The coalition of citizens that sought to establish community colleges as "democracy's colleges" hoped to create higher education institutions that would welcome all learners, especially from their local communities. People imagined places free from a hierarchy of knowing that arbitrarily favors one kind of learning over another. They imagined comprehensive institutions where continuing education, adult basic education, English as a Second Language, developmental education, university transfer, and professional and technical programs would be on an equal footing—the opportunities for cross-fertilization and collaboration among diverse educators and students, a genuine benefit of teaching and learning. In some respects, the "invigorated, practical liberal arts education" as described in *Greater Expectations* is not so different from citizens' initial hopes for the pluralistic student learning they imagined would happen in higher education, especially for community colleges. They imagined places that would increase the social mobility of minority and working-class students, their sons and daughters.

The role learning communities can play in the high stakes endeavor of preparing students for an education of quality—if these efforts are scaled up and become an initiative embraced by an entire institution—is a conversation worth pursuing and a practice worth doing. When you go to the Pasadena City College's Teaching and Learning Communities Program, whether in person or virtually, you will be greeted by a wonderful motto: "The classroom door is open: imagine the possibilities." Students do. It is our work to figure out how we can support and challenge students—and ourselves—so they can meet our greater expectations while realizing their own.

Endnotes

1. UW-Seattle is 74 percent white, 19 percent Asian, 3 percent Hispanic, 2 percent black, and 1 percent other; EWU is 80 percent white, 4 percent Asian, 3 percent Hispanic, 2 percent black, and 11 percent other; and SCCC is 48 percent white, 17 percent Asian, 9 percent Hispanic, 13 percent black and 13 percent other.
2. High school exit exams are used by *no* state to determine whether students need developmental classes, a telling fact regarding the alignment between K-12 exit standards and college entrance requirements.
3. Findings from this study undertaken by Kathleen Byrd and Kathy Harrigan are summarized in a handout, *Narrative: Common Themes and Concerns, 2002.*
4. In its first year the group awarded $300,000 in scholarships, grants, and stipend monies to "support students' dreams." In 2003, 32 students will receive over $2,000,000 in awards.

References

Abraham, A. A. 1987. *A Report on College-Level Remedial/Developmental Programs in SREB States.* Atlanta: Southern Regional Education Board.

Adelman, C. 1998. "The Kiss of Death? An Alternative View of College Remediation." *National Crosstalk* 6(3): 11. San Jose, CA: National Center for Public Policy and Higher Education.

Adelman, C. 1999. *Answers in the Tool Box: Academic Intensity, Attendance Patterns, and Bachelor's Degree Attainment.* Washington, DC: U.S. Department of Education, Office of Educational Research and Improvement.

Adler, M., and C. Van Doren. 1972. *How to Read a Book.* New York: MJF Books.

Alverno College Faculty. 1994. *Student Assessment-as-Learning at Alverno College.* Milwaukee, WI: Alverno College.

Alverno College Faculty. 2000. *Self Assessment at Alverno College*, G. Loacker, ed. Milwaukee, WI: Alverno College.

Anderson, J. D. 1988. *The Education of Blacks in the South: 1860-1935.* Chapel Hill: University of North Carolina Press.

Arendale, D. 2002. "History of Supplemental Instruction (SI): Mainstreaming of Developmental Education." In *Histories of Developmental Education.* by D. B. Lundell and J. Higbee, eds. Minneapolis, MN: Center for Research on Developmental Education and Urban Literacy, General College, University of Minnesota.

Association of American Colleges and Universities. 2002. *Greater Expectations: A New Vision for Learning as a Nation Goes to College.* Washington, DC: Association of American Colleges and Universities.

Astin, A. W. 1985. *Achieving Education Excellence: A Critical Assessment of Priorities and Practices in Higher Education.* San Francisco: Jossey-Bass.

Astin, A. 1993. *What Matters in College: Four Critical Years Revisited.* San Francisco: Jossey-Bass.

Bailey, T. 2001. *Community Colleges in the 21st Century: Challenges and Opportunities.* New York: Community College Research Center, Teachers College, Columbia University.

Barr, R. B., and J. Tagg. 1995. "From Teaching to Learning: A New Paradigm for Undergraduate Education." *Change* 27: 12-25.

Book, W. F. 1927. "How Well College Students Can Read." *School and Society* 26(669), August: 242-48.

Boylan, H. R. 1995. "The Scope of Developmental Education: Some Basic Information on the Field." *Research in Developmental Education* 11(2): 1-4.

Boylan, H. R. 2002. *What Works: Research-Based Best Practices in Developmental Education.* Boone, NC: Continuous Quality Improvement Network with the National Center for Developmental Education.

Boylan, H. R., B. Bonham, L. Bliss, and C. Claxton. "The State of the Art in Developmental Education: Report of a National Study." Paper presented at the First National Conference on Research in Developmental Education, Charlotte, NC, November 1992.

Boylan, H. R., and D. P. Saxon. 1998. "The Origin, Scope and Outcomes of Developmental Education in the 20th Century." In *Developmental Education: Preparing Successful College Students.* J. Higbee and P. Dwinell, eds. Columbia, SC: National Center for the First-Year Experience and Students in Transition, University of South Carolina.

Boylan, H. R., and W. G. White Jr. 1987. "Educating All the Nation's People: The Historical Roots of Developmental Education." Pt.1, *Research in Developmental Education* 4(4-5): 1-4.

Brier, E. 1984. "Bridging the Academic Preparation Gap: An Historical View." *Journal of Developmental Education* 8(1): 2-5.

Brint, S., and J. Karabel. 1989. *The Diverted Dream: Community Colleges and the Promise of Educational Opportunity in America, 1900-1985.* New York: Oxford University Press.

Brubacher, J. S., and W. Rudy. 1976. *Higher Education in Transition: A History of American Colleges and Universities 1636-1976*. New York: Harper-Collins.

Bruffee, K. A. 1986. "Social Construction, Language, and the Authority of Knowledge: Bibliographical Essay." *College English* 48(8), December: 773-90.

Callan, P., et al. 2000. *Measuring Up 2000: The State By State Report Card on Higher Education*. Wichita, KS: National Center for Public Policy and Higher Education. Also available online at http://measuringup.highereducation.org/2000/reporthome.htm.

Casazza, M. 1998. "Strengthening Practice with Theory." *Journal of Developmental Education 22(2)* Winter: 1-11.

Casazza, M., and S. Silverman. 1996. *Learning Assistance and Developmental Education: A Guide for Effective Practice*. San Francisco: Jossey-Bass.

Christ, F. L. 1997. "The Learning Assistance Center as I Lived It." In *Proceedings of the 15th and 16th Annual Institutes for Learning Assistance Professionals:1994 and 1995*. S. Mioduski and G. Enright, eds. Tucson, AZ: University Learning Center, University of Arizona.

Collins, T. 2002. Foreword to *Histories of Developmental Education*. D. B. Lundell and J. L. Higbee, eds. Minneapolis, MN: Center for Research on Developmental Education and Urban Literacy, General College, University of Minnesota.

Collins, T., and D. V. Taylor. 2000. Foreword to *Proceedings of the First Intentional Meeting on Future Directions in Developmental Education*. D. B. Lundell and J. L. Higbee, eds. Minneapolis, MN: Center for Research on Developmental Education and Urban Literacy, General College, University of Minnesota.

Community College Survey of Student Engagement. 2002. *Engaging Community Colleges: A First Look*. www.ccsse.org/publications/report.pdf.

Continuous Quality Improvement Network (CQIN)/American Productivity and Quality Center (APQC). 2000. *Benchmarking Best Practices in Developmental Education*. Houston, TX: American Productivity and Quality Center.

Cromwell, L., T. Riordan, and S. Slocum. 2002. "Thriving in Academe: Taking Responsibility for Student Learning." *Advocate: National Education Association* 19(4), April: 4-7.

Cross, K. P. 1971. *Beyond the Open Door: New Students to Higher Education*. San Francisco: Jossey-Bass.

Cross, K. P. 1976. *Accent On Learning: Improving Instruction and Reshaping the Curriculum*. San Francisco: Jossey-Bass.

Dahlgren, L. O. 1984. "Outcomes of Learning." In *The Experience of Learning*. F. Marton, D. Hounsell, and N. Entwistle, eds. Edinburgh: Scottish Academic Press.

Donovan, R. 1974. *National Project II: Alternatives to the Revolving Door*. Bronx, NY: Bronx Community College.

Dougherty, K. J. 1994. *The Contradictory College: The Conflicting Origins, Impacts, and Futures of the Community College*. Albany, NY: State University of New York Press.

Downing, S. 2002. *On Course: Strategies for Creating Success in College and in Life*. 2nd ed. New York: Houghton Mifflin College.

Dropkin, R., and A. Tobier, eds. 1976. *Roots of Open Education in America: Reminiscences and Reflections.* New York: The Workshop Center for Open Education.

Duranczyk, I. M., and J. Caniglia. 1998. "Student Beliefs, Learning Theories, and Developmental Mathematics: New Challenges in Preparing Successful College Students." In *Developmental Education: Preparing Successful College Students.* J. L. Higbee and P. L. Dwinell, eds. Columbia, SC: National Resource Center for The First-Year Experience and Students in Transition, University of South Carolina.

Dweck, C. S. 2000. *Self-Theories: Their Role in Motivation, Personality, and Development.* Philadelphia, PA: Psychology Press.

Education Commission of the States. 2002. *State Policies on Community College Remedial Education: Findings from a National Survey.* Denver, CO: Center for Community College Policy.

Education Trust. 1998. *Education Watch: The Education Trust 1998 State and National Data Book.* Washington, DC: Education Trust.

Entwistle, N. 2000. "Promoting Deep Learning Through Teaching and Assessment." In *Assessment to Promote Deep Learning: Insights from AAHE's 2000 and 1999 Assessment Conferences.* L. Suskie, ed. Washington, DC: American Association for Higher Education.

Finkel, D. L. 2000. *Teaching With Your Mouth Shut.* Portsmouth, NH: Heinemann.

Fogarty, J., L. Dunlap, et al. 2003. *Learning Communities in Community Colleges.* National Learning Communities Project Monograph Series. Olympia, WA: The Evergreen State College, Washington Center for Improving the Quality of Undergraduate Education, in cooperation with the American Association of Community Colleges and the American Association for Higher Education.

Fox, T. 1999. *Defending Access: A Critique of Standards in Higher Education.* Chico, CA: California State University.

Freire, P. 1970. *Pedagogy of the Oppressed.* New York: Herder and Herder.

Gibbs, G. 1992. *Improving the Quality of Student Learning.* Bristol: Technical and Educational Services.

Gleazer, E. J. 1970. "The Community College: Issues of the 1970's." *Educational Record* 51: 47-52.

Grastie, K. 1998. "Greenville Technical College and Kaplan Learning Services: A Joint Partnership for Creating Successful Innovations in Developmental Studies." In *Developmental Education: A Twenty-First Century Social and Economic Imperative.* R. H. McCabe and P. R. Day Jr., eds. Mission Viejo, CA: League for Innovation in the Community College and the College Board.

Grubb, W. N., and Associates. 1999. *Honored But Invisible: An Inside Look At Teaching in Community Colleges.* New York: Routledge.

Hardin, C. H. 1998. "Who Belongs in College? A Second Look." In *Developmental Education: Preparing Successful College Students.* J. Higbee and P. Dwinnel, eds. Columbia, SC: National Center for the First-Year Experience and Students in Transition, University of South Carolina.

Higbee, J. L., and P. L. Dwinell, eds. 1998. *Developmental Education: Preparing Successful College Students*. Columbia, SC: National Resource Center for The First-Year Experience and Students in Transition: University of South Carolina.

Hill, Patrick. 1985. "The Rationale for Learning Communities." Speech given at the Inaugural Conference on Learning Communities by the Washington Center for Improving the Quality of Undergraduate Education, The Evergreen State College, Olympia, WA.

Hill, P. 1991. "Multi-Culturalism: The Crucial Philosophical and Organizational Issues." *Change* 23 (4): 38-47.

Horton, M., and P. Freire. 1990. *We Make the Road by Walking: Conversations on Education and Social Change*. B. Bell, J. Gaventa, and J. Peters, eds. Philadelphia: Temple University Press.

Karabel, J. 1972. "Community Colleges and Social Stratification: Submerged Class Conflict in American Higher Education." *Harvard Educational Review* 42: 521-562.

Kates, S. 2001. *Activist Rhetorics and American Higher Education 1885-1937*. Carbondale, IL: Southern Illinois University Press.

Kidd, J. R. 1973. *How Adults Learn*. New York: Cambridge Press.

Kiemig, R. 1983. *Raising Academic Standards: A Guide to Learning Improvement*. Washington, DC: Association for the Study of Higher Education, Educational Resource Information Center.

Kluger, R. 1975. *Simple Justice*. New York: Vintage Books.

Knowles, M. S. 1970. *The Modern Practice of Adult Education: Andragogy Versus Pedagogy* New York: Association Press.

Knowles, M. S., E. F. Holton, and R. A. Swanson. 1998. *The Adult Learner: The Definitive Classic in Adult Education and Human Resource Management*. Houston, TX: Gulf Publishing Company.

Koolsbergen, W. 2001. "Approaching Diversity: Some Classroom Strategies for Learning Communities" *Peer Review*, Summer/Fall: 25-31.

Kozol, J. 1991. *Savage Inequalities: Children in America's Schools*. New York: Harper Collins.

League for Innovation in the Community College. 1990. *Serving Underprepared Students*. Laguna Hills, CA: League for Innovation in the Community College.

Lardner, E. Decker, and others. Forthcoming. *Learning Communities and Diversity*. National Learning Communities Project Monograph Series. Olympia, WA: The Evergreen State College, Washington Center for Improving the Quality of Undergraduate Education, in cooperation with the American Association for Higher Education.

Lundell, D. B., and J. L. Higbee, eds. 2000. *Proceedings of the First Intentional Meeting on Future Directions in Developmental Education*. Minneapolis, MN: Center for Research on Developmental Education and Urban Literacy, General College, University of Minnesota. Also available online at http://www.gen.umn.edu/research and click on CRDEUL.

MacGregor, J. 1990. "Collaborative Learning: Shared Inquiry as a Process of Reform." In *The Changing Face of College Teaching*. M. D. Svinicki, ed. New Directions for Teaching and Learning Series, 42, Summer. San Francisco: Jossey Bass.

Malnarich, G. 1994. *". . . whiz into the future": Learner Agency and Teaching Adults Reading*. Burnaby: Simon Fraser University.

Malnarich, G., and E. Decker Lardner. 2003. "Designing Integrated Learning for Students: A Heuristic for Teaching, Assessment, and Curriculum Design." Washington Center for Improving the Quality of Undergraduate Education Occasional Paper, Winter, no. 1.

Martin, D. C., and D. Arendale. 1994. *Supplemental Instruction: Increasing Achievement and Retention*. New Directions in Teaching and Learning, 60. San Francisco: Jossey-Bass.

Marton, F., D. Hounsell, and N. Entwistle, eds. 1984. *The Experience of Learning*. Edinburgh: Scottish Academic Press.

Marton, F., and R. Säljö. 1984. "Approaches to Learning." In *The Experience of Learning*. F. Marton, D. Hounsell, and N. Entwistle, eds. Edinburgh: Scottish Academic Press.

Maxwell, M. 1979. *Improving Student Learning Skills: A Comprehensive Guide to Successful Practices and Programs for Increasing the Performance of Underprepared Students*. San Francisco: Jossey-Bass.

Maxwell, M. 1997. *Improving Student Learning Skills: A New Edition*. Clearwater, FL: H & H Publishing Company, Inc.

Maxwell, M. 1998. "A Commentary on the Current State of Developmental Reading Program." In *Developmental Education: Preparing Successful College Students*. J. L. Higbee, and P. L. Dwinell, eds. Columbia, SC: National Resource Center for The First-Year Experience and Students in Transition: University of South Carolina.

McCabe, R. H. 2000a. *No One to Waste: A Report to Public Decision-Makers and Community College Leaders*. Washington, DC: Community College Press.

McCabe, R. H. 2000b. "Underprepared Students." In response to *Measuring Up 2000: The State By State Report Card on Higher Education*. Wichita, KN: National Center for Public Policy and Higher Education.

McCabe, R. H. 2003. *Yes We Can! A Community College Guide for Developing America's Underprepared*. Phoenix, AZ: League for Innovation in the Community College and Washington, DC: American Association of Community Colleges.

McCabe, R. H., and P. R. Day Jr., eds. 1998. *Developmental Education: A Twenty-First Century Social and Economic Imperative*. Mission Viejo, CA: League for Innovation in the Community College and The College Board.

Moses, R., and C. E. Cobb Jr. 2001. *Radical Equations: Civil Rights from Mississippi to the Algebra Project*. Boston, MA: Beacon Press.

National Center for Education Statistics. 1991. *College Level Remedial Education in the Fall of 1989*. Washington, DC: U.S. Department of Education.

National Center for Education Statistics. 1996. *Remedial Education at Higher Education Institutions, Fall 1995*. Washington, DC: U.S. Department of Education, Office of Educational Research and Improvement.

National Center for Public Policy and Higher Education. 2002. *A National Status Report on the Affordability of American Education*. San Jose, CA.

National Survey of Student Engagement 2002 Annual Report (www.indiana.edu/ ~nsse/html/nsse-2002.shtml)

Noel, L., R. Levitz, D. Saluri, and Associates. 1985. *Increasing Student Retention: Effective Programs and Practices for Reducing the Drop Out Rate*. San Francisco, CA: Jossey-Bass.

O'Banion, T. 1997. *A Learning College for the 21st Century*. Washington, DC: American Association of Community Colleges, American Council on Education Series on Higher Education: Oryx Press.

Perry, W.G. 1970. *Forms of Intellectual and Ethical Development in the College Years: A Scheme*. New York: Holt, Rinehart, and Winston.

Pratt, M. L. 1991. "Arts of the Contact Zone." *Profession* 91, 33-40. New York: MLA.

Ramsden, P., ed. 1988. *Improving Learning: New Perspectives*. London: Kogan Page.

Ramsden, P., D. G. Beswick, and J. A. Bowden. 1986. "Effects of Learning Skills Interventions on First-Year University Students' Learning." *Human Learning* 5: 151-64.

Ratcliff and Associates. 1995. *Realizing the Potential: Improving Postsecondary Teaching, Learning, and Assessment*. University Park, PA: National Center on Postsecondary Teaching, Learning, and Assessment.

Rhoads, R. A., and J. R. Valdez. 1996. Democracy, *Multiculturalism, and the Community College: A Critical Perspective*. New York: Garland.

Rogers, C. R. 1951. *Client-Centered Therapy*. Boston: Houghton-Mifflin.

Rogers, C. R. 1969. *Freedom to Learn*. Columbus, OH: Merill.

Rossman, J. E., et al. 1975. *Open Admissions at the City University of New York: An Analysis of the First Year*. New York: Prentice Hall.

Roueche, J. E. 1968. *Salvage, Redirection, or Custody?* Washington, DC: American Association of Junior Colleges.

Rouche, J. E., G. A. Baker, and S. D. Rouche. 1984. *College Responses to Low-Achieving Students: A National Study*. Orlando, FL: HBJ Media Systems.

Roueche, J. E., and S. Roueche. 1993. *Between a Rock and a Hard Place: The At-Risk Student in the Open Door College*. Washington, DC: Community College Press.

Roueche, J. E., and S. Roueche. 1999. *High Stakes, High Performance: Making Remedial Education Work*. Washington, DC: American Association of Community Colleges.

Schilling, K. M., and K. L Schilling. 1999. "Increasing Expectations for Student Effort." *About Campus* May/June: 4-10.

Shaw, K. M. 1997. "Remedial Education as Ideological Battleground: Emerging Remedial Education Policies in the Community College." *Educational Evaluation and Policy Analysis* 19(3): 284-296.

Shaw, M. E. 2002. "Recovering the Vision of John Dewey for Developmental Education." In *Histories of Developmental Education*. D. B. Lundell and J. L. Higbee, eds. Minneapolis, MN: The Center for Research on Developmental Education and Urban Literacy, General College, University of Minnesota.

Smilkstein, R. 2002. *We're Born to Learn: Using the Brain's Natural Learning Process to Create Today's Curriculum*. Thousand Oaks, CA: Corwin Press.

Smith, B. L., and J. McCann, eds. 2001. *Re-Inventing Ourselves, Interdisciplinary Education, Collaborative Learning, and Experimentation in Higher Education*. Bolton, MA: Anker Publishing Company.

Smith, B. L., J. MacGregor, R. Matthews, and F. Gabelnick. Forthcoming. *Learning Communities: Reforming Undergraduate Education*. San Francisco: Jossey-Bass.

Spann Jr., M. G., and S. D. McCrimmon. 1998. "Remedial/Developmental Education: Past, Present, and Future." In *Developmental Education: Preparing Successful College Students*. J. L. Higbee and P. L. Dwinell, eds. Columbia, SC: National Resource Center for The First-Year Experience and Students in Transition: University of South Carolina.

Spear, K., et al. 2003. *Learning Communities in the Liberal Arts Colleges*. National Learning Communities Project Monograph Series. Olympia, WA: The Evergreen State College, Washington Center for Improving the Quality of Undergraduate Education, in cooperation with the American Association for Higher Education.

Sprout, A. L. 1990. "Do U.S. Schools Make the Grade?" *Fortune*, Spring: 50-51.

Steen, L. A. 2001. *Mathematics and Democracy: The Case for Quantitative Literacy*. Princeton, NJ: National Council on Education and the Disciplines, The Woodrow Wilson National Fellowship Foundation.

Stoll, E. 1999. "Interdisciplinary Learning Communities at De Anza College: Moving from the Margins Toward the Mainstream." In *Strengthening Learning Communities: Case Studies from the National Learning Communities Dissemination Project (FIPSE)*, by J. MacGregor et al. Olympia, WA: The Evergreen State College, Washington Center for Improving the Quality of Undergraduate Education.

Svensson, L. 1984. "Skill in Learning." In *The Experience of Learning*, F. Marton, D. Hounsell, and N. Entwistle, eds. Edinburgh: Scottish Academic Press.

Tagg, J. 2003. *The Learning Paradigm College*. Bolton, MA: Anker Publishing Company.

Taylor, K., B. Moore, J. MacGregor, and J. Lindblad. 2003. *Learning Community Research and Assessment: What We Know Now*. National Learning Communities Project Monograph Series. Olympia, WA: The Evergreen State College, Washington Center for Improving the Quality of Undergraduate Education, in cooperation with the American Association for Higher Education.

Tinto, V. 1987. *Leaving College: The Causes and Cures of Student Attrition*. Chicago: University of Chicago Press.

Tinto, V. 1995. "Learning Communities, Collaborative Learning, and the Pedagogy of Educational Citizenship." *AAHE Bulletin*, March: 11-13.

Tinto, V. 1997. "Classrooms as Communities: Exploring the Educational Character of Student Persistence." *Journal of Higher Education*, 68(6): 599-623.

Tinto, V., A. G. Love, and P. Russo. 1993. "Building Community." *Liberal Education*, Fall:16-21.

Tinto, V., A. G. Love, and P. Russo. 1994. "Building Learning Communities for New College Students: A Summary of Research Findings of the Collaborative Learning Project." Washington, DC: National Center of Postsecondary Teaching, Learning, and Assessment; Office of Educational Research and Improvement; U.S. Department of Education.

Trow, M. A. 1983. "Underprepared Students at Public Research Universities: Maintaining Access and Standards." *Current Issues in Higher Education* 1: 16-26.

United States Department of Education. 1991. *Historically Black Colleges and Universities and Higher Education Desegregation*. Washington, DC: Office of Civil Rights.

van Slyck, P. 1997. "Repositioning Ourselves in the Contact Zone." *College English* 59(2), February: 149-70.

Williams, J. 1990. "Marshall's Law." In *Eight Men and a Lady: Profiles of the Justices of the Supreme Court*. O'Brien, ed. Bethesda, MD: National Press.

Wittman-Grahler, V. 2002. "Math is for Everyone!" *Washington Center News*, Fall. Olympia, WA: Washington Center for Improving the Quality of Undergraduate Education, The Evergreen State College.

Wyatt, M. 1992. "The Past, Present, and Future Need for College Reading Courses in the U.S." *Journal of Reading* 36(1), September: 10-20.

Zwerling, L .S. 1976. *Second Best: The Crisis of the Community College*. New York: McGraw-Hill.

II

Section Two

Learning Community Case Studies
Drawing Lessons Early On:
The Learning Community Factor in Teaching and Learning
Ben Sloan, Fayetteville Technical Community College

In the past I would have students disappear without a word. Sometimes ones with "A" averages would drop, and I would try to call them to find out what the problem is, all to no avail.

—Jerry Ittenbach, Chemistry

Located in south-central North Carolina about an hour south of Raleigh, Fayetteville Technical Community College (FTCC) serves 13,000 college students as well as 26,000 continuing education students annually, with one-third of all curriculum students taking at least one developmental class each semester. Many students who come to this large urban school have been displaced from textile industry jobs due to plant closings. Many others are associated with the military since two large bases, Fort Bragg and Pope Air Force Base, are nearby. The demographics of Raleigh contribute to an unusually high level of student diversity at FTCC; those eligible for education benefits include current enlistees from around the country, retirees, and spouses from many foreign countries, including Korea and Germany, where the United States maintains large military bases.

Learning communities are relatively new to FTCC: the first two offered in the spring of 2001, and six now offered in the fall of 2003. Most of the original five instructors teaching in learning communities since their inception began working together in 1993 under the auspices of a large College Tech Prep grant-funded effort that emphasized the development of interdisciplinary teaching strategies. The idea to develop learning communities originated with two faculty members who attended learning community-related conferences and workshops. The instructors involved from the beginning are Jerry Ittenbach, Chemistry; Beverly Hall, Math; Chris Diorietes, Math; Vicki Pate, Sociology and Humanities; and Ben Sloan, English.

The two original learning communities were developmental math/developmental chemistry and developmental English/sociology. Because developmental math and developmental chemistry were two difficult-to-pass courses for students wishing to enter a health-related field, integrating the courses in the context of health-related activities and discussions would help students succeed in each. This learning community is now offered every semester and fills to capacity. The second learning community, offered every spring semester, combines developmental English and sociology, a popular elective and transfer-credit course for many different curricula at FTCC. The expectation was that the two courses would complement one another: the sociology context would add energy and excitement to an otherwise routine developmental writing course, while the writing would challenge students to think and communicate on a deeper level about sociology.

The expectation was that the two courses would complement one another: the sociology context would add energy and excitement to an otherwise routine developmental writing course, while the writing would challenge students to think and communicate on a deeper level about sociology.

The Developmental Math/Developmental Chemistry Learning Community

The learning community combining a sixteen-week Introductory Algebra course with two, eight-week Basic Chemistry I & II courses is taught back-to-

Outside class, most students meet with their group members on a daily basis to work together on assignments and projects, a trend that instructors do everything in their power to encourage.

back, for a total of twelve contact hours—a full schedule for most students. For these instructors, the preeminent value of the learning community class over traditional stand-alone classes is *retention*. In a typical stand-alone chemistry class at FTCC, by mid-semester one-third of the students drop out, and by the end of the semester it is not unusual for half or more to have dropped. In a typical stand-alone math class, one quarter of the students are gone by mid-semester, and by the end it is not unusual for a third or a half of the students to have dropped. By comparison, typically 80 percent or more finish the semester with a passing grade in the math/chemistry learning community.

Part of the problem with chemistry is that students hear such scary stories that many give up before they start. Furthermore, once these students—most of whom have never had chemistry before—arrive in the class, a serious stumbling block is that they cannot "do" algebra. For math students who ask "what is this math stuff good for?" and "when will I ever use this?," the learning community gives them an opportunity to see direct applications for algebra in career fields.

One strategy that addresses retention is the use of "Support Circles," carefully contrived groups of four to five students organized on the basis of mixed ability or skill level, compatible out-of-class study time schedules, and shared "interests" such as childcare and transportation-related needs. In fact, much of what the students do in class involves Support Circle-related work; students bounce ideas off one another in a setting where they hear encouraging words from peers so no one will be in danger of feeling lost or isolated. Outside class, most students meet with their group members on a daily basis to work together on assignments and projects, a trend that instructors do everything in their power to encourage. One student who was on the verge of quitting wrote the following at the end of the semester:

> Coming back to school did not seem possible and fear encompassed my very being . . . Everyone's ability to learn is different, for various reasons, but being given the chance for 16 weeks to see the same faces, and talk the same talk, somewhat forces a greater bond of dependence of one [student] on the other. The learning community won't allow absolute failure.

The learning community helps to disentangle challenging assignments, such as ones that involve combining percentages of different chemical concentrations to come up with a chemical of intermediate strength. From the perspective of math, students often say, "It's a word problem; I can't do it." A simulated pharmaceutical research activity, however, asks students to become research technicians for an invented pharmaceutical company. The assignment focuses on the importance of mixing chemicals in just the right amount to create a desired product. As students proceed, the role of algebra becomes quite apparent to them.

In a stand-alone math class a student might be frustrated by attempting to analyze information, build equations, and then solve the equations; in the learning community setting students are mixing the chemicals and using lab equipment to verify what they come up with on paper. Students get practical information at the same time they learn a process they will use later in their chosen health-career field. In addition, students' learning is deeper when abstract ideas are linked with concrete experiences and when group members work together throughout the activity. Another assignment that enhances "bonding" among students is a Chemical Scavenger Hunt where group members go off campus to "find" chemicals and then provide their full names, formulas, and product names.

In practice, the math/chemistry learning community has proven to be a superb way to capitalize on the diversity that students bring to the classroom. Faculty also appreciate that developmental students are fragile and can benefit by becoming cheerleaders for one another. Food plays an important role when celebrating the successful completion of projects or special occasions such as Pi Day and Mole Day. For example, recently before touring a local hospital to learn about health-related careers, students and instructors met for breakfast at a nearby restaurant. The aim is to take advantage of every possible opportunity to help students feel comfortable with one another.

The Developmental English/ Sociology Learning Community

Vicki Pate from the Sociology Department and I teach in the second learning community first offered in 2001. This learning community combines the highest-level developmental writing course, English 90 (Composition Strategies) with a college-transfer-level Introduction to Sociology class. The purpose for blending these courses is to create an effective learning environment for students. Writing topics and exercises need to relate to the need for citizens to communicate clearly with one another about controversial, complex social issues. Students also need not simply to memorize theories and terms but to challenge themselves to apply concepts to real-life situations and then articulate their findings in class discussions and in writing. Because I already attempted to make writing more meaningful for students by asking students to communicate about their life experiences as they relate to social conflict and because Vicki required writing in her classes to deepen their engagement with sociological concepts, the courses were a natural fit for a learning community.

Like many colleges across the country, FTCC uses ACCUPLACER to make a writing class placement based on scores derived from "Reading Proficiency" and "Sentence Skills" multiple-choice questions rather than an evaluation of the student's original writing based on a reading prompt. Students placed in writing classes based solely on their performance on multiple-choice-type questions often have a much better ability to articulate their experiences and ideas than the assessment instrument scores would seem to indicate. Learning communities provided an avenue for demonstrating that students could do better.

How the learning community operates

Case studies in the learning community become the occasion for mastery of sociological concepts and terms through classroom discussion as well as writing essays. When working on a case study, students first read about and then discuss a puzzling, unresolved situation. For example, one case study concerns a mother who relocates to the United States from a remote South American village. She brings her young daughter into a community health clinic to be evaluated by a nurse whom she has visited on previous occasions. When the nurse notices a curious pattern of bruises and cuts, the mother explains that the child seemed to lack energy so the family performed a native-to-their-own-culture tribal "cure." The nurse chooses not to communicate the situation to her supervisor, opting instead to rely on her evolving closeness with the young woman as the basis for eventually attempting to convince her that in the United States such "cures" may represent child abuse and could result in a child being taken away from parents. The question for the students is this: Did the nurse make the right decision?

The case studies we choose illustrate sociological concepts explained in the students' textbook. At the same time that students are reading the case studies and preparing to discuss them in class, they are also reading chapters in a sociology textbook that explain various concepts such as social interaction, stratification, and the sociological imagination. During the discussion of the case study, students refer in their textbooks to particular terms and theories. We act as facilitators, recorders, and guides with respect to the exchange on various issues, terms, and concepts. We also pose questions and participate in the ongoing dialogue so that students can discover the connections between concrete, specific case studies and sociological theory. The discussion culminates with each student taking and defending sides of an issue, in writing. The students know in advance they will write argument essays defending their positions based on the sociological material in their textbooks.

After students work together in peer sessions to develop and improve their essays, they submit their papers, along with all earlier drafts, for an "initial" evaluation. Vicki and I discuss each paper together, and complete a one-page evaluation that addresses strengths and weaknesses in the areas of content, organization, and grammar. The student uses these comments to revise the paper for inclusion in a culminating portfolio, submitted at mid-term or the end of the semester, that contains several papers for which the student will receive one grade. As a result of the combined case study/portfolio approach, student papers generally convey thinking at a deeper level and involve more complex ideas than are typically found in papers produced in stand-alone composition classes.

Students also work on a semester-long project, done individually or in groups, called "Stories of American Community." This assignment, taking the place of a conventional research paper, requires students to investigate in their community a specific, unique point of social conflict and the means being attempted to resolve the conflict. The students conduct their investigations through interviews and document the experience with black-and-white photographs. For example, one student who wrote a paper on a local women's center support group interviewed not only the counselor but also several participants. Another student reported on the attempts of the Lumbee Indians to gain recognition as a tribe; her photographs showed a local swamp where a famous skirmish took place, burial sites, and the inside of relatives' homes decorated in the Native American style. A third student interviewed a county commissioner who offered insight into local government politics. When the projects are completed, students present their results in an oral report to the entire class; they also submit a typed report that is evaluated and returned for revision and final submission using the portfolio format.

The learning community setting helps the sociology instructor achieve the primary goal for the students in any Introduction to Sociology class, which is to grasp the concept of the sociological imagination—for each student to see beyond his or her self into a larger, more diverse world. Everything Vicki does centers on this goal, and students' writing demonstrates whether they are able to apply sociological concepts to their own experience as well as the experience of others.

Conclusion

Teachers in learning communities at Fayetteville Technical Community College have been changed by the experience. We carry the lessons from our learning community experiences into teaching in stand-alone classes in ways that emphasize:

- *community-building strategies,* which make it easier for students to work together and support one another, both academically and personally
- *writing versus traditional objective tests to measure learning* so students can experience writing as a means to stretch, focus, and deepen their thinking
- *facilitating instead of lecturing* since active engagement in learning encourages students to discover, individually and through group work, the academically-appropriate questions to ask and processes to use to answer their questions
- *creative and innovative approaches and activities* that spark student interest and open possibilities for student learning unavailable through traditional means
- *collaborating with teachers from other disciplines*, a value, that once discovered, benefits students and faculty if pursued in practice. Opening a dialogue with a teacher from a different department that results in shared activities or a full-blown learning community creates opportunities for significant professional growth

Website: http://www.faytechcc.edu
Contact: Ben Sloan, bsloan@pvcc.edu
Learning Community Coordinator: Vicki Pate, patcv@faytechcc.edu

Learning More, Learning Better:
Developmental and ESL Learning Communities

Phyllis van Slyck, LaGuardia Community College, City University of New York

You learn to think, re-think, and even re-re-think in the different classes. You not only learn more this way, you learn better.

–LaGuardia student

. . . the most important kind of support we offer incoming students occurs through our learning communities.

LaGuardia Community College is located in Long Island City, Queens, just over the Queensborough Bridge from Manhattan. Queens itself is one of the most ethnically and economically diverse boroughs in New York, possibly in the United States, and LaGuardia's student profile mirrors this diversity. Its students come from every borough of New York City, and from more than 140 different countries. Nonetheless, LaGuardia students have a number of things in common with students attending public community colleges around the country. The median age of LaGuardia students is about twenty-two, and many are working class (64 percent have an annual income of $25,000 or less) and are the first in their family to attend college. Only 38 percent of entering students come directly from high school; 47 percent are already working. In an incoming survey, these students express concern about their ability to perform well in college and 80 percent are worried about having enough time to keep up with their studies. This is understandable since 45 percent have jobs, 63 percent of those work more than twenty hours a week, and almost 20 percent have children, two-thirds of whom are under six years of age.

In terms of academic preparation, 91 percent of incoming LaGuardia students need at least one developmental course; however, in the last few years an increasing number of students are placed into ESL courses rather than basic writing courses (1999-2000: 23 percent to 35 percent). As of 2001, 65 percent of new students are foreign born and 49 percent of these students have been in the United States for less than five years. Many, but not all, foreign and immigrant students read and write in their native language proficiently and a large number do not use English outside of the LaGuardia classroom.[1] Given the complex skills issues suggested by this information and competing demands on working students with family obligations, concern about success in college is clearly justified.

LaGuardia faculty and administrators have addressed the needs of entering students through an array of First Year experiences including a daylong introduction to the college with workshops (Opening Sessions) taught by faculty, a common reading, mentoring services, and new student seminars.[2] We also offer end-of-semester, one-week intensive courses in Basic Writing (English Express) and Basic Math (Second Chance) for students who have failed these courses but are close to passing. But perhaps the most important kind of support we offer incoming students occurs through our learning communities.

A primary way LaGuardia has sought to create community and enhance support for ESL and developmental students in particular is through its New Student House program, first piloted and assessed in 1992, and targeting our most at-risk incoming students, those who need basic skills courses in three areas: reading, writing, and speech. Our goal has been to create a fully coordinated learning experience and foster a sense of belonging for students who have not traditionally felt connected to academic life and who face competing demands of family and work.

The New Student House, in its original configuration, consisted of the three developmental courses Basic Reading, Basic Writing, and Oral Communication and a Freshman Seminar taught by a counselor. (All developmental courses at LaGuardia include an additional weekly hour of tutoring in writing, reading, and speech labs.) The original House consisted of three "apartments," each with a cohort of twenty-five students. This meant that teaching in the house constituted a full schedule for each faculty member (each taught three sections of the developmental course). It was also a complete schedule for the students. This structure made it possible to have individual "apartments" with different levels of the Basic Writing and Basic Reading courses. One apartment, for example, was taught with a six-hour version of Basic Writing and Essentials of Reading I; another was taught with a four-hour version of Basic Writing and Essentials of Reading II. Placement into these sections depended on testing results, but one unique advantage to the program was that students could be moved around during the semester and thereby given additional support according to their individual needs. Faculty teaching in the house met regularly with the counselor to evaluate student progress, and decisions were made on a weekly basis about the kind of support each student needed. The flexibility and individual attention offered by the structure of the program and the collaboration and dialogue of the faculty and counselor were essential to the success of the original program.

Since participation in the New Student House Program is voluntary, a little needs to be said about how students are selected and the role of faculty in initial recruitment and support. Institutional research helps us identify students who would place into this program and an individual letter, followed by a phone call, is sent to each student. In this letter, students are given a snapshot of the program, including a block schedule (four days 9:00 a.m.-3:00 p.m.) that they would be unable to duplicate taking these courses separately. The letter includes an invitation to a special day of advisement and registration for the program—a short-cut through registration for basic skills students who must meet with an advisor. On this day, faculty teaching in the program are on hand to meet students, answer questions, and describe the integrated curriculum they have planned together. This registration and advisement day is very important in the message it sends to these students: yes, LaGuardia has 11,000 students and you are part of an incoming class of 3,000, but you are special and we will give you the individual attention you need—on your first day, and throughout your first semester.[3]

One semester prior to teaching in the learning community, faculty meet to plan an integrated curriculum. They agree on common readings, choose films and field trips, and develop a joint syllabus. When possible, this coordinated curriculum includes sequenced and/or simultaneous assignments based on these common materials so the materials and activities from one discipline can serve as a resource for work in another. Coordinated activities are developed and refined throughout the semester. In one program, for example, the reading professor assigned Richard Wright's *Native Son* so the Writing and Speech professors designed parallel writing assignments and activities to deepen students' understanding of the themes and issues raised by the novel. The speech professor, for example, led his students in preparing a trial of the main character, Bigger

Our goal has been to create a fully coordinated learning experience and foster a sense of belonging for students who have not traditionally felt connected to academic life and who face competing demands of family and work.

Thomas, and divided the three apartments of the House into prosecution, defense, and jury, with individual students volunteering to play the main characters. The writing professor created a parallel argumentation assignment (including research into the democratic system) in which students had to defend their position regarding Bigger Thomas's guilt or innocence. A culminating event for the semester was an actual staging of the trial. In an end-of-term evaluation of the program, one student wrote, "I learned how to speak in public for the first time without being afraid," and another said, "The best thing about the New Student House was when all three classes got together and made a show."

Faculty teaching in the House stress not only the importance of curriculum integration but also the need for ongoing dialogue and flexibility. Faculty have many anecdotes about the team support necessary to effect a change in plans. One English professor remembers asking other members of the teaching team to give up a group film viewing and discussion because students were anxious about a recently returned writing assignment and needed more time for revision. Not only did the other faculty members agree to postpone the film, they asked the English professor how they could help and, together, reading, speech, and writing instructors designed activities directly related to the writing assignment. This was a moment when students as well as faculty members felt powerfully supported.

Faculty teaching in the House meet on a weekly basis to evaluate the effectiveness of their curriculum and pedagogy, and to discuss the needs of individual students. (It should be noted that faculty teaching in a House for the first time receive, when possible, an hour of release time for this collaboration.) The counselor who teaches the Freshman Seminar plays an essential role in this ongoing evaluation by administering early and later self-assessment assignments to students and by attending one or more classes taught by the reading, writing, and speech faculty and giving these instructors—and the students—feedback. The counselor might suggest, for example, that the instructor vary her pedagogy to reach students whose learning style is more visual; in his own Freshman Seminar he might make observations about the importance of note-taking or participating in the group. In an end-of-term evaluation, one faculty member notes, "We wouldn't have been able to give focused and consistent support to our most at-risk students without the help of a counselor teaching in the program."

In its first year, Vincent Tinto, a professor of education and sociology at Syracuse University, conducted a study to assess whether the goals of the program were being met. The primary goals were to increase the retention and success of developmental students. Our data showed a 15-20 percent higher retention rate one and two semesters beyond the learning community and a substantially higher pass rate in individual courses.[4] (In the English course, which is the most difficult to pass, House students achieved a 24 percent higher pass rate in 1992 and a 33 percent higher pass rate in 1994, compared to students taking these courses separately.) But the program was also successful for both faculty and students in unanticipated ways. The students' experience in the learning community strengthens their engagement in and commitment to the college community beyond the classroom and many become involved in student government and clubs.[5] In responding to end-of-semester surveys, a high

"We wouldn't have been able to give focused and consistent support to our most at-risk students without the help of a counselor teaching in the program."

percentage commented on the community that was created by the House, including a recognition of the encouragement and support they received in each of their classes, benefits of small and large group activities, an appreciation of close relationships developed with teachers, an awareness of intellectual links among the different courses, and an increased confidence in their writing and their ability to speak in large groups. Finally, many students commented on the importance of friendships developed and asked about participating in future learning communities.[6]

Faculty, too, had an overwhelmingly positive response to working in the House but warned of the intensity of the experience. As is often the case with truly integrated learning community work, they noted the value of in-depth dialogue with colleagues about pedagogy and curriculum, the creativity and excitement of synthesizing ideas and classroom practice in team-taught sessions, and the importance of ongoing evaluation of student progress, so that the most at-risk students were receiving the kind of support typical of much smaller private colleges rather than a large public institution. Reflecting on the level of engagement necessary to work effectively in the program, some faculty suggested that one should not teach in the House for two consecutive semesters. The initial team and several subsequent teams stressed the importance of faculty members choosing their own teams and having adequate planning time before teaching together. Some faculty also emphasized the need for extreme availability and attentiveness to student needs and indicated that this kind of teaching is not for everyone. Overwhelmingly, students in this kind of developmental program have had in the past less than positive educational experiences: they may have experienced repeated failure in high school; poor work habits and study skills may interfere with their ability to focus in class or complete homework assignments; and self-esteem issues may make them especially fragile. Seasoned and flexible faculty who are willing to evaluate student progress and adjust their pedagogy to meet individual student needs are essential to the success of the program.

Since 1994, the New Student House at LaGuardia has replaced one of its basic skills courses (Oral Communication) with a college-level version of that course, and we have experimented successfully with other college-level courses such as Introduction to Business, Introduction to Computers, and Reading Biography.[7] During the 2002-03 academic year, a Basic Skills Task Force met to consider how to build on the success of LaGuardia's learning communities and reach a larger population. One result is a new pilot of Freshman Academies, which is in the planning stages. Its goal is to offer two basic skills courses and a college-level course in the major to virtually all developmental students in that major. The first two pilot majors for these academies will be Business and Computer Science, two of our most popular majors for incoming students.

A year after the original New Student House was piloted, an ESL faculty team designed a new version of the program: a two-apartment house, each with a six-hour ESL course, a speech course (Communication for the Non-Native Speaker), Essentials of Reading I or II (one in each apartment), and a New Student Seminar. This faculty team chose "Immigration" as its theme and designed a complete joint syllabus with common texts and articles, research

The students' experience in the learning community strengthens their engagement in and commitment to the college community beyond the classroom and many become involved in student government and clubs.

projects on issues such as illegal aliens, conflicts between cultural tradition and American law, intercultural relationships, jobs filled by immigrants, and a field trip to Ellis Island. Having worked together for more than six years, the faculty team recently redesigned their curriculum around the theme of "Women's Issues and Women's Rights," with research projects on the history of women's rights in America and globally.

In terms of curriculum content and advancing the skills levels of students, one clear benefit (in addition to overall higher retention and pass rates) is that the synthesis of activities across disciplines enables students to engage in deeper analytic tasks than would be possible in a stand-alone basic skills course.

In addition to their version of the New Student House, the ESL Program at LaGuardia has been working steadily for more than a decade to support ESL students and provide them with college-level courses. Currently, 50 percent of the highest-level ESL courses are paired with 100 level colleges courses in a variety of disciplines including business, accounting, computer science, sociology, theatre, and human services. ESL faculty have initiated many of these pairs, seeking out faculty in a discipline that interests them and designing ESL readings and assignments directly related to the discipline. ESL faculty speak enthusiastically of the satisfaction they derive from working with faculty in other disciplines and of the immense benefits for students. A recent ten-year study shows that ESL students are outperforming non-ESL students taking these college-level courses independently.

Based on learning community work for more than twenty years, LaGuardia faculty and administrators have recommendations, concerns, and goals for future learning communities, especially for developmental and ESL students. First and foremost, LaGuardia faculty feel strongly that these learning communities work best when they are faculty driven, that is to say, when faculty choose their own teams and design their integrated curriculum. They are most successful when faculty are engaged in recursive evaluation of student progress and of their own curriculum and pedagogy, in individual classes and in linked activities and assignments. Essential to this is adequate time for planning and evaluation before and during the semester the learning community is taught (and, whenever possible, some compensation for this work in the form of released time or a stipend).

In our developmental learning communities, faculty speak powerfully about the importance of the counselor, and, whenever possible, a New Student Seminar taught by the counselor is attached to each of these learning communities. When faculty teams are meeting regularly and the counselor has the opportunity to visit their classes, he or she has the opportunity to help the whole team recognize and support the most at-risk students. Early intervention for these students, including additional tutoring, and the concentrated awareness and support of the faculty team can make all the difference in these students' success in the program. In terms of curriculum content and advancing the skills levels of students, one clear benefit (in addition to overall higher retention and pass rates) is that the synthesis of activities across disciplines enables students to engage in deeper analytic tasks than would be possible in a stand-alone basic skills course.[8]

While faculty and administrators feel that developmental and ESL learning communities at LaGuardia have been highly successful in the last decade particularly, and our institutional data supports this conclusion, a major goal is to expand these offerings for a larger cohort of incoming students. (Currently a two-

or three-apartment house serves only fifty to seventy-five students.) Within our incoming class each fall of approximately 1,500 students, more than 90 percent need at least one developmental course. We need to expand the learning community offerings so that a majority of these students can benefit from the level of integration and support offered in such programs as the New Student House. Perhaps in another year we will be able to report on the effectiveness of the Academy model piloted in the spring of 2004.

Website: http://www.lagcc.cuny.edu
Contact: Phyllis van Slyck, vanph@lagcc.cuny.edu

Endnotes

1. Data on LaGuardia student diversity and skills are taken from the Institutional Profile. For more detailed information, see our website: www.laguardia.edu/facts/archives/facts2001.
2. In 2003 The Policy Center on the First Year of College, a national research center funded by The Pew Charitable Trusts and The Atlantic Philanthropies with a basic mission to improve the first year of college, selected LaGuardia as an "Institution of Excellence in the First College Year." LaGuardia was among thirteen institutions nationwide chosen from a field of 130 nominees through a competitive selection process.
3. The procedure described in this paragraph has evolved and been modified as more registration moves online and as pre-freshman summer immersion programs have expanded at LaGuardia. There are now a variety of ways students learn about and enter developmental and other first-year clusters.
4. Data on pass rates in individual courses in the House continue to suggest that learning outcomes can be directly related to the learning community experience. Data on retention have varied from semester to semester. A 2002 survey indicates that the majority of students who drop out do so for reasons completely external to college life (for financial or family reasons).
5. We have not been able to document consistently higher retention in the House but do have data supporting higher pass rates in the developmental courses in the learning community.
6. For a booklet on the New Student House, including program design, data on retention and success, and student and faculty interviews, contact Phyllis van Slyck, English Department, LaGuardia Community College, vanph@lagcc.cuny.edu.
7. This change was implemented in part because of changing financial aid regulations in New York: incoming students need at least one college-level course to qualify for financial aid.
8. For an example of this kind of research-oriented activity in the ESL New Student House, contact Rashida Aziz, ESL Credit Program, azizra@lagcc.cuny.edu.

College Knowledge:
Creating Meaningful Preparatory Curriculum
Pam Dusenberry, Shoreline Community College

Throughout my life I have always hated reading . . . Now I see my problem was understanding what I was reading, not reading itself. The reading log process forced me to comprehend what I was reading, by finding the main points and writing them down.

—A student

All forms of reading, especially in a college setting, benefit from using writing to process information in the form of notes, summaries, reflections, responses, reporting, and research writing.

Shoreline Community College (SCC) just north of Seattle, serves 8,000 students. Approximately half the students are working toward transferring to a four-year institution and the other half toward a professional-technical degree or certificate. About 25 percent of the student body is from various U.S. co-cultures and from other countries; 75 percent are white, as are half the students in Developmental English.

In the early 1990s, two English faculty decided to recreate the Developmental English program to address underprepared students' needs. As part of a Title III grant, we reviewed literature in cognitive psychology, linguistics, reading theory, adult education, and other fields relevant to helping students become strong learners. The result is a three-course learning community sequence that differs significantly from traditional developmental programs in several ways.

Probably the most apparent difference in SCC's Developmental English sequence is that reading, writing, and study skills are integrated at all levels. All forms of reading, especially in a college setting, benefit from using writing to process information in the form of notes, summaries, reflections, responses, reporting, and research writing. In fact, writing is the clearest way that students' reading process can be made apparent for evaluation, metacognitive awareness, and improvement. Conversely, reading provides models for writing as well as the source of material for writing. At the same time, reading and writing are also major tools for learning—two important elements of study skills. The fact that most developmental programs do not provide students with the opportunity to practice skills in college-like contexts could contribute to perennially low retention rates among underprepared students.

A second feature of the Developmental English sequence is that students read college-level material and practice a reading process every time they read (Dusenberry et al. 2002). Our review of the literature indicated that students needed to hone their reading, writing, and thinking abilities using materials they encounter later in their college studies. Traditionally, reading instruction for college students, especially those deemed underprepared, has had students learn discrete reading skills such as identifying main ideas and details, defining vocabulary, and so on, in short selections or excerpts that are often not related to each other.

In our sequence, we assign challenging, college-level readings for three reasons. First, students develop and practice reading of a difficulty similar to what they will encounter in their college classes. Second, students learn a reading process that includes distinguishing more important from less important information (finding main ideas) and identifying words they don't understand. Third, the content is carefully chosen to help students understand college culture and the academic subjects. The readings are related in meaning and build on each other; they help students develop a deeper understanding of ideas and their relationships that serve their current and later learning.

Students have a difficult time comprehending reading for two general reasons: they don't have sufficient background knowledge, including vocabulary and context, and they don't have adequate or appropriate strategies to attack the reading. If students learn a functional reading process including strategies for solving reading problems, and they are given adequate background knowledge, they can understand even very difficult material. Another tangible result of choosing challenging material is the pride that students feel in their intellectual accomplishments.

Rather than providing teacher-generated pre-reading and post-reading questions, we teach students a consistent reading process called a Reading Log, which requires readers to follow an eleven-step process: pre-reading to get ready to learn, reading to understand and to learn, and post-reading to consolidate learning. Students use their Reading Logs to identify issues, questions, confusions, and problems for discussion. At first, students do not like this assignment, but come to appreciate the difference it makes in their ability to understand and remember what they read.

Just as students practice the whole reading process in all three courses of the sequence, they also compose essays in all three courses. Because segmenting part of the writing process is not effective, this practice in composing whole essays regularly is productive. Relationships among the concepts of thesis, organization, and development are extremely complex so continual writing enables students to focus on depth, heart, and style.

Finally, and perhaps the most important difference, readings of essays, articles, stories, poems, and textbook chapters in the courses occur around themes of "college culture." As critical thinking leader Richard Paul (1993) says, students must have something to think critically *about*. Providing readings of increasing complexity all related to one common theme helps students build deep understanding and critical thinking abilities that cannot be taught or practiced without depth of knowledge. Through readings about what it means to be educated and what kinds of thinking and problem solving are valued in the academy, students can practice reading on meaningful materials while gaining knowledge that can help them write more sophisticated and meaningful essays.

The transition to college from homemaking, high school, or the working world is a tremendously difficult one. This difficulty is not due primarily, however, to an inability to think critically, write grammatically, or develop appropriate study habits. The most important factor in successfully making the transition into college is the ability to adjust to the culture shock students experience when they enter the academic world. The Developmental English sequence helps students understand, appreciate, and utilize the unique culture of that academic world. This acculturation means learning about the values, behaviors, and sanctions of the academy. Students need to be introduced to these values in an analytical and critical environment so they can evaluate their benefits and freely choose to participate in the culture of college.

The readings are related in meaning and build on each other; they help students develop a deeper understanding of ideas and their relationships that serve their current and later learning.

For example, in Critical Thinking in College and Life, the first course in SCC's Developmental English program, students read short fiction and essays about the transition to college and the qualities of successful learners among other things: "I never knew that you could read all about a person's life experience like this. I never knew you could write about it, either." The student who makes these comments has just read *The Magic Barrel* by Bernard Malamud, and the class discusses it in a unit on the role and effects of family culture on life choices. In light of the Malamud story and other readings, students talk together about how their families' and cultures' attitudes about education affect their choices about college, and how their own experiences compare to the author's experiences. Their written and spoken comments are insightful, and despite a few spelling and grammar errors, are cogent and understandable. In addition to learning about the role that culture plays in life, students work on close reading, summarizing, interpreting, note taking, and group process abilities.

In the middle-level course, College Culture and Thought, students learn the concepts of culture, norms, and values. From that foundation, readings then introduce students to the many experiences of the members of the campus community. In one reading, author Earl Shorris introduces a sociological view of why people have such a hard time escaping poverty. He argues that poor people do not need simple job training; instead, they benefit from a rigorous, traditional course in the Humanities: history, philosophy, logic, and the arts. Students grapple with Shorris' ideas; some classes choose to read Plato's *Allegory of the Cave* because Shorris mentions it as important to his students' learning. For some students, the metaphor of the cave is a way to understand their own life situations and their goals for education. Readings such as this one introduce students to the culture of the college community and invite them to analyze, evaluate, and use those cultural elements.

Students also often lack an understanding of the academic organization of knowledge and the basic concepts of the disciplines that are bound up in hidden rules, codes, and discourses. What counts as evidence in a chemistry paper, for example, is different than what counts as evidence in a literary analysis. Each discipline takes a specialized approach to studying the world. Readings provide discussions of the key issues within a discipline and provide specific examples of thinking within disciplines. At the end of any or all of the three reading- and writing-intensive developmental courses in the SCC sequence, students have a much more complete picture of what they are getting into in college as well as improved reading, writing, thinking, and learning skills.

To conclude, SCC's developmental program is based on seven principles:
1. Students need to read whole college-level texts.
2. They need to see the connections between the abilities and content they learn and their present and future lives.
3. They need to understand the values and organizational systems that permeate college life.
4. They need content that helps them learn important background knowledge about college culture and the disciplines.
5. They need to engage in the consideration of big ideas.

6. They need to develop confidence by reading (and composing) intellectually challenging, sophisticated texts.
7. They need to be expected to think and learn like the adults they are.

Website: http://www.shore.ctc.edu/shoreline
Contact: Pam Dusenberry, pdusenbe@shoreline.edu

References

Dusenberry, P., D. Henry, and T. Rody. 2002. *College Knowledge: Entries into Academic Culture.* Shoreline Community College, WA: Kendall Hunt Publishing Co.

Paul, R. W. 1993. "The Logic of Creative and Critical Thinking." In R. Paul, *Critical Thinking: How to Prepare Students for a Rapidly Changing World*, 195-215. Santa Rosa, CA: Foundation for Critical Thinking.

Learning How to Learn:
A Foundation for Developmental Learning Communities
Jan Swinton, Spokane Falls Community College

While participating in these paired courses, I not only came to terms with my biases regarding the sciences, I also came to terms with myself. I discovered that I was capable of achieving in the sciences.

— A student

Our learning community program for developmental learners focuses on learning strategies that will help students become effective learners in the multiple contexts of college-level and developmental courses.

Spokane Falls Community College, located in a metropolitan area in eastern Washington, is a commuter college with 5,700 students, 80 percent of whom are full-time. The student population tends has the average age of approximately twenty-six years; 11 percent are students of color and 1 percent are international students.

In 1990, Spokane Falls Community College (SFCC) offered its first learning community that integrated three transfer-level courses. Today, our typical fall quarter schedule includes a coordinated studies offering and twelve paired and linked courses. Since our learning community program's inception, developmental level skills courses, paired or linked with a content course or another developmental course, have been a significant component. In particular, developmental learning communities have focused on helping students learn— about specific subject areas, about their community, and about themselves as learners.

While we want students to use the skills they learn in our study strategies classes in other areas of school and their lives, transfer rarely happens. Our learning community program for developmental learners focuses on learning strategies that will help students become effective learners in the multiple contexts of college-level and developmental courses. The majority of our offerings include a reading and/or study-strategies course paired with a course such as Introduction to Biology or Elementary Algebra, as well as core courses in professional/technical programs such as Early Childhood, Deaf Interpreter, and Gerontology.

SFCC's paired courses integrate two or more courses, which are fully team-taught, with faculty participating as learners as well as teachers. A cohort of students, usually forty, registers for a particular section of a study strategies course and a particular section of a content class. The students meet with both instructors present for a two-hour block each day; sometimes, the learning community includes a lab.

The first learning-to-learn pairing, "Biology: How to Study It and How to Write About It," integrated a developmental study skills with a transfer-level biology class. This pairing came about when a life science instructor approached me with her concerns about her biology students' reading and writing abilities. They struggled with their complex textbook, which like most introductory science textbooks, is written for expert, not novice, readers. Much to her students' dismay, she required them to read *Never Cry Wolf* and write an essay (they couldn't imagine having to write an essay in a biology class!). This conversation took place just as I was learning about learning communities, and combining study skills with biology seemed an excellent way to support this instructor and her students. I had no idea how much it would change the way I taught study-strategies classes.

A Washington Center seed grant funded reassigned time so I could attend the biology class to prepare for the pairing of my study skills course with Biology 101. My role was much like that of the master student in a supplemental instruction model. I attended all lecture and lab classes, took notes, read the assignments, prepared for, and took the tests. By participating in the biology class with a focus on how to learn the subject, I learned a great deal about the *real* world of studying and learning. My colleagues and I realized that to be effective developmental educators, we needed to be in conversations with content faculty and in classes other than our own, discovering the realities with which students struggle.

I learned what it was like to be a student with a desire to learn but little time to study. Before the first biology test, I *intended* to review my notes and other materials every night. Since I am a developmental learner in life sciences, when I did *not* practice daily, I had to study eight hours the day before the test. Suddenly, daily study sessions became a priority. Likewise, even though I was using my best listening and note-taking practices, it was hard to keep new information from "bouncing off" me—each lecture brought a great deal of new information, and terms from the previous day were used to define that day's new concepts. I needed mental time-outs every fifteen to twenty minutes to process what I had just heard and to check my understanding. These insights helped shape the activities I designed for future quarters to ensure that students monitored their learning and reviewed lecture material daily.

The two-hour block on lecture days gave the biology instructor more time to lecture on complex concepts. We broke the lectures into twenty to thirty minute chunks; in between, students engaged in activities that helped them think through the information they had just heard. They compared lecture notes, collaborated on key words or questions, and then orally tested each other. Early in the quarter students were urged to form study groups outside of class. When the encouragement to form groups proved ineffective, we held in-class reviews in my portion of class time, focusing on effective strategies for group work. An earlier suggestion to form a study group outside of class "before the next test," now became a study skills course requirement. Students reported that required group work was one of the most effective activities in helping them learn.

While a traditional biology text is required, students created their own resource notebooks of study strategies, handouts, and materials relating to time management and test-taking instead of purchasing a "study skills" textbook. I carry the lesson I learned in this first paired course—that a skills textbook could be replaced with the students' own resource notebook— to most subsequent learning communities. Students monitored their learning by completing weekly journal assignments on topics such as their learning difficulties and successes, study habits, and attitudes. We also assessed the latter two with Claire Ellen Weinstein's e-LASSI, an electronic *Learning and Study Strategies Inventory*.

By practicing new and various study strategies, students were better able to learn biology; likewise, a difficult-to-master content provided students with extra incentive to try new strategies and learn about themselves as learners. It was enormously rewarding, then, to read what Joe, a forty-year-old nursing student

Students reported that required group work was one of the most effective activities in helping them learn.

who had failed biology the previous quarter, wrote in his journal: "by using all of these methods and doing the group study and these methods, I *know* I learned biology."

Learning to learn does more than help students pass a course; it can also open doors previously closed to them. Such was the case with Regina Corkery, an English major who opened what she thought had been a locked door when she discovered she was capable of "learning" science:

Learning to learn does more than help students pass a course; it can also open doors previously closed to them.

> Prior to taking the combined courses, I had no thought of taking any more science classes than were absolutely required of me to gain an associates degree and get on to a more palatable field of study. I had a biased view of the sciences, anyone who achieved in them, and anyone who pursued them . . . sciences were for a certain breed of people—namely those with extraordinarily high I.Q.s or photographic memories . . . (but) biology became fascinating to me, and breaking my old self-image opened up new avenues for me. After completing this combined course, I signed up for more science courses . . . I decided to change to a major requiring a significant science background: nursing . . . I attribute (this) experience with cracking a terrible myth for me that I know many others are struggling with.

Once the other reading instructors and I turned our focus outward, we realized that recent hires in some of SFCC's professional/technical programs were eager for our help in teaching their students critical reading and study skills, and organizational and literacy skills required in the workplace. We paired the study strategies course with Interpersonal Communications, a course required by most Human Services professional/technical programs. Because of the range in students' reading and writing skills when they enter Human Services programs, we offer two levels of the study skills course: a transfer (elective) course for students with reading skills at or above college level, and a developmental course for students with below college-level reading scores. Students do basically the same curriculum but at a different proficiency level.

In the professional/technical learning communities, the need for assistance from a counselor was clear early on. We incorporated a service-learning component in a paired study skills/Interpersonal Communications learning community by adding a two-credit Human Services Seminar. While this seminar did not require additional in-class time, students did ten hours of service learning plus reflection. SFCC's Service Learning Coordinator, who has a counseling background, coordinated the component, worked individually with students, and referred them to other resources in the community. Based on this experience, we want to build counseling support into other developmental learning communities.

SFCC's linked classes are those in which faculty coordinate syllabi and assignments, but usually teach their classes separately. We have linked a study strategies course with content courses such as Elementary Algebra, Early Childhood Development, Gerontology, and Deaf Culture. We have also linked a reading/study skills course to a lecture-centered course, which has a twenty-student capacity, and each course counts as one class for each instructor.

Generally, the reading/study skills instructor receives compensation or reassigned time to sit in on the content course the first time the link is offered to determine which study strategies to emphasize.

The lessons we have learned about the importance of providing an authentic context for learning various study and reading strategies is borne out in the research. Learners do not naturally transfer information or concepts where we most expect this transfer to take place: school knowledge to everyday practice; sound everyday practice to school endeavors; and across school subjects. As Sue Berryman and Thomas Bailey (1992) indicate in "Five Incorrect Assumptions About Learning," the most prevalent incorrect assumption is that people predictably transfer learning to new situations. Another incorrect assumption is that knowledge and skills can be more readily transferred to new situations if they are acquired independent of use. The reality, though, is that *context* is critical for understanding and for learning. Integrated courses give students practice applying the new study strategies they are learning in a content field.

L. Dee Fink (2002) notes that we need to focus on *what* students learn as well as the changes that occur in the learner. Combining study strategy courses with content classes focuses on what Fink describes as *a change in connecting*. For Fink, connecting is "the ability to connect and integrate, for example, different kinds of information and ideas with each other, classroom learning with other parts of one's life, etc." (2). When students are involved in interdisciplinary work, they make connections and deepen their learning. Vincent Tinto's retention study on students in learning communities reveals that developmental education students are 26 percent more successful in their studies if they are involved in integrated courses (1997).

The success students experienced when we focused on strategies to help them learn particular subjects led us to offer a paired developmental level reading and writing learning community and a linked reading and writing LC each year. Whether linked or paired, College Survival is a ten-credit program that helps students improve their understanding of what they read and their ability to communicate ideas orally and in writing. Class activities are designed to prepare students for English 101 and for professional/technical or transfer-level academic programs. Throughout the quarter students reflect on themselves as learners and discover their learning preferences; they leave the learning community with this self-awareness as well as a personal study plan for future quarters.

A comprehensive assessment of SFCC's learning community program from spring 1997 to spring 1999 indicates that students were satisfied with their learning community experience and felt it important to their success. They increased their confidence in reading and writing, developed a deeper understanding of course content, and recognized their responsibility for their learning. A 2000 SFCC Outcomes study in the professional/technical division shows that students in the Interpreter Training program who successfully completed a study skills course in conjunction with Deaf Culture persist longer and are more successful in the Interpreter Training program than students who do not take the linked study skills course.

The success students experienced when we focused on strategies to help them learn particular subjects led us to offer a paired developmental level reading and writing learning community and a linked reading and writing LC each year.

Teachers of developmental courses use multiple strategies to promote active student learning, and these strategies become a permanent part of the content teachers' repertoires.

For SFCC faculty members, students' success has not been the only reward of teaching together in learning communities. Participating in another instructor's class, preferably in an area outside one's own discipline provides content teachers with sustained faculty development. Teachers of developmental courses use multiple strategies to promote active student learning, and these strategies become a permanent part of the content teachers' repertoires. For example, after the first paired biology and study skills course, the biology instructor began spending more time at the beginning of the quarter engaging students in community building and time management activities that helped students get acquainted and plan for the necessary two hours of study outside of class for every hour in class. She also periodically provides more pre-reading assignments (such as survey maps of the biology chapters that the students also later use as review maps from which to study) and active learning assignments such as flashcards that portray biology terms and concepts with definitions and student illustrations. To teach basic chemistry concepts early in the quarter, she assigned jigsaw group work in which students become "experts" on a concept by working collaboratively with others assigned to the same concept, then, in turn, they "teach" their original group.

Teaching in learning communities elucidates the applicability of course material. Pairing my course with another course forced me to reassess the most critical elements of the study skills curriculum. I found that some study strategies that I usually taught in my study skills course, such as SQ3R, were not efficient or effective for learning biology. Similarly, the Gerontology instructor and I discovered that many goals of the learning skills course address important but unarticulated expectations of the professional/technical instructors and future employers. Through their study skills assignments, students learned and practiced organization, responsibility, and reliability—invisible but essential parts of their curriculum. In subsequent quarters, the Gerontology instructor has been much more explicit about teaching these habits. Instructors in the Interpreter Training program have modified the way they teach summary writing. Students now have guided instruction and support from the reading instructor as they work at understanding and summarizing ideas. As a result, we are seeing better comprehension and more accurate written summaries.

Our learning communities continue to change and evolve. We face new challenges as budgets are reduced and more students with significant learning problems enroll in our college. However, we steadily move forward and offer the following suggestions for other colleagues interested in creating learning communities that focus on students learning how-to-learn:

a) Pair or link developmental skills courses with a high demand course that students are likely to need for a degree or certificate since students may opt for the learning community solely because it enrolls them in the required course.

b) Choose a course taught by an instructor committed to improving student learning who wants to participate in a learning community. Pairing or linking a course with someone else's involves more planning and preparation than teaching a stand-alone course. Ask for a commitment

from your colleague(s) to meet outside class time at least one hour each
week to debrief, plan, and adjust your plan.

c) Involve a counselor in your learning community. Many schools add a one
to two credit career planning course that counselors teach as a way to
involve the counselor. Another possible format is to assign a counselor to a
developmental level learning community as a part of his/her contact time.

Website: http://www.sfcc.spokane.cc.wa.us
Contact: Jan Swinton, jans@spokanefalls.edu

References

Berryman, S. E., and T. R. Bailey. 1992. *The Double Helix of Education and the Economy*. Teachers College Press: Columbia University.

Fink, L. D. 2002. *Higher Level Learning: A Taxonomy for Identifying Different Kinds of Significant Learning*. Professional and Organizational Development Network in Higher Education. Retrieved July 8, 2003, from http://ase.tufts.edu/cae/tufts-secure/v11/v11n2.htm.

Tinto, V. 1997. "Classrooms as Communities: Exploring the Educational Character of Student Persistence." *Journal of Higher Education*. 68(6), November/December: 599-623.

LEARNING COMMUNITIES MONOGRAPH SERIES
The Pedagogy of Possibilities: Developmental Education,
College-Level Studies, and Learning Communities

99

Learning Community Snapshots

General Education First Year Cluster Program:
California State University, Hayward

I have taught freshman for twenty-five years and when I started seeing the richness and knowledge base students bring to their writing in a cluster, I was stunned. So often students just "exercise" their way through a freshman writing class; they are completely unengaged . . . I think we get such good work from the students because the clusters are challenging and students rise to the occasion because they remain steeped in their topic, their theme.

—Alison Warriner

Since the fall of 1998, all first-time students in the California State University (CSU) system who do not score 550 or better on their SATs must take an English Placement Test (EPT) and an Entry Level Mathematics Test (ELM) before admission. In the CSU system, students whose EPT and ELM placement results identify them as "remedial students" cannot enroll in any other courses until they register for appropriate remedial courses. These must be taken in the first quarter and in subsequent quarters until students are prepared for baccalaureate-level English and/or Mathematics courses. Students are allowed only one repeat of required coursework and they need to meet CSU system requirements within one-year.

At California State University, Hayward, 55 percent of 750 entering freshmen do not meet the cut-off writing score and 60 percent fall below the needed score in mathematics. Unlike open admission community colleges, Cal State Hayward receives no budget allocation to support underprepared students. Many of these students whose placement results identify them as "remedial students" stand in the top one-third of their high school class. They have completed college preparatory coursework with a GPA that qualifies them for admission. Misaligned expectations explain some of these results—for instance, high school English focuses on literature and not argumentative writing, a college-level expectation. Unfortunately, a successful outreach program where college and high school teachers work together to articulate what students need to know for college entry has recently been cut.

In these circumstances, the General Education First Year Cluster Program continues to be an ambitious and successful program with a forward-looking approach that addresses entering students' various levels of academic preparation without marginalizing those who are compelled to take developmental courses. At Cal State Hayward, all freshmen students choose for the first three quarters of their undergraduate education from more than a dozen clusters of thematically linked courses in the natural sciences, arts and humanities, or social sciences. These cluster classes connect students and professors who share similar interests in a learning community that links courses, with many opportunities for curricular integration, based on a common theme or inquiry. For instance, the "How Things Work" cluster offered in fall quarter 2003 through Spring Quarter 2004, introduces the shared theme to students in this way: "Have you ever wondered how a bicycle or a light bulb works? How humans exercise and use their senses? How earthquakes and volcanoes occur? If you're curious about how science explains how things work this cluster is for you." Biology, geology, and physics are the three discipline courses in the cluster, one of which is taken each quarter. Another cluster, "Viewing Diversity," connects coursework in anthropology, ethnic studies, and communication, the common element a critical overview of "some of the most important issues pertinent to a broad variety of ways in which human beings perceive diversity. Major emphasis will be devoted to visual presentations of diversity regarding individual identity, culture, gender, race, ethnicity, nationality and the global balance of political and economic power." Developmental students can register for all clusters except classes in the sciences that specify admission requirements.

Each quarter, students take one of three thematically-linked discipline-based courses tied to an information literacy class taught by a librarian, along with classes in English composition, speech, and an academic success component that is taught by lecturers and graduate students. Each quarter a general education (GE) activity course ties cluster classes together. Within the English composition component, students enroll in different writing courses based on their writing ability. For instance, in fall quarter 2002, approximately 120 to 130 students were enrolled in English 0989, a tutorial led by faculty for no more than ten students who place just below college-level writing proficiency; around 100 students enrolled in a writing 0804 course designed for non-native speakers whose writing ability placed them at a "college ready" level; and, the program also ran more than fifteen sections of a three-quarter 0801, 0802, and 0803 developmental writing course sequence for native speakers.

While mathematics is not part of a learning community cluster, the progress of students who enroll in developmental level mathematics courses, in addition to the General Education Cluster Program, is tracked. The academic success component includes an introduction to campus resources, academic counseling, and learning and study skill strategies that support students not only in their cluster classes, but also in learning math. Academic advisors and counselors attend academic success classes and students can participate in a peer-mentoring program.

While many factors combine to create a successful cluster program, the composition component of the clusters is taught by a highly trained group of instructors who are part of the Cal Sate Hayward composition program, praised by an external reviewer and writing-across-the-curriculum expert as one of the best composition communities in the country. Many instructors who teach developmental writing are graduates of or graduate students in the composition program where they receive training on working with developmental students along with seminars on writing pedagogy. For instance, beginning graduate students take the theory and practice of composition in fall quarter, followed by a writing-across-the curriculum course in winter quarter, and a spring practicum on teaching writing where they shadow an experienced developmental instructor for the entire quarter and also student teach for a few weeks in a developmental composition class. When these graduate students begin to teach in the Cluster Program, they have experience and are further supported by several organized meetings throughout each quarter where instructors who teach developmental writing students, including those who are part-time, share materials and offer one

Another cluster, "Viewing Diversity," connects coursework in anthropology, ethnic studies, and communication, the common element a critical overview of "some of the most important issues pertinent to a broad variety of ways in which human beings perceive diversity.

another support. Writing teachers design the writing curriculum based on the books and syllabi used in the cluster and consult other cluster writing faculty that may include up to three developmental teachers and one to two faculty who teach college level English.

At the end of their freshmen year, students whose entry assessment results require them to take three quarters of developmental math and three quarters of developmental English typically complete a total of forty-four credits, twenty-four of which are remedial and twenty are baccalaureate units.

Website: http://www.csuhayward.edu
Coordinator: Sally Murphy, smurphy@csuhayward.edu

Learning in Communities (LinC) Program: De Anza College

I appreciated the multiple perspectives and more meaningful contexts that two teachers and an integrated curriculum provides

—De Anza student

De Anza College's 24,000 students commute from a ninety-mile radius to take courses at a college known for its record of student success in certificate, degree, and transfer programs. Located in Cupertino, in the heart of the Silicon Valley, De Anza's student body reflects various diversities—ethnic, class, gender, and educational preparation. Students are from more than eighty different countries, and 57 percent are people of color. New students are required to take an English placement test as well as basic skill tests in math and, depending on their program, in chemistry and biology. Eighty percent of these students place in developmental reading, writing, and math classes. Although the college's entering students are among the most underprepared in the Californian system, 1,800 De Anza students transfer to four-year public institutions each year, double the average transfer rate for California community colleges. The college is also among the top three community colleges in the country that award associate degrees.

The Learning in Communities (LinC) Program, established in fall 1997, has evolved from an array of interdisciplinary classes that began in the mid- to late-1980s in Language Arts and the accelerated Honors Program. Language Arts (LART), for instance, has offered integrated reading and writing links for developmental students for more than a decade. The curricular integration varies, as does the teaching format: links are taught by a team; by two instructors who teach individually, but adopt a common theme and share some assignments; or by one instructor. Despite severe budget cutbacks, the college has created five new LARTs to meet the needs of developmental students. In fall 2003 offerings included "America Reloaded: Reading and Writing in the New Millennium" (LART 100-Reading 100/English Writing 100b) and "Issues of Our Times: Personal Courage, Violence in Society, and Family Relationships" (LART 200-Reading 201/English Writing 100A).

Each academic quarter, De Anza students can choose from an average of ten different learning communities. Given that the majority of entering students place in developmental classes, most links, clusters, and cohorts are developmental or are combinations of developmental and general education courses. In fact, a major emphasis of the LinC program has been to foster curricular connections between developmental and general education courses. This approach reflects a broader institutional goal, the timely and successful transition of students from developmental to college-level courses. For instance, entering students who do not qualify for English composition can enroll in Summer Express, a six-week summer learning community that integrates classes in pre-college reading, writing, and college orientation. By fall, 90 to 95 percent of these students typically meet entrance requirements. The institutional commitment to student success means that faculty work closely with counselors who offer learning community students special office hours and counseling. Some LARTs are also linked to counseling. For instance, a LART 100 learning community, "Tabloid Trash, The Real World and You: Surviving and Succeeding on the Road to English 1A," includes a counselor in the three-person teaching team.

The curricular integration varies, as does the teaching format: links are taught by a team; by two instructors who teach individually, but adopt a common theme and share some assignments; or by one instructor.

Expectations and guidelines for designing, implementing, and assessing learning community curriculum are explicit; faculty who want to teach in a learning community are supported by workshops and in-service professional development.

For students completing entrance requirements, earning college credit at the same time is motivating. The LinC Program offers two approaches to integrating pre-college classes with college-level general education courses. The first approach clusters courses around the linked developmental reading and English curriculum. For instance, in "Comics Speak Our Lives: The Graphic Novel Meets English 1A," the developmental link is clustered with Arts 1A, an Introduction to the Visual Arts (this course has also been linked to developmental-level math). "Looking In, Speaking Out: Our Impact on Fashion and Consumerism" links developmental reading and writing and their respective labs with Speech Communications. Other versions link developmental classes to history, English literature, sociology, accounting, and business. The second approach combines a large lecture class with embedded cohorts, often in composition. This model was introduced by a political science instructor who invited English instructors to "merge" with his large Power and Voice lecture class to create three cohorts that would regroup from 25 to 50 students in ESL, Developmental English, or college-level English classes. A version has been adapted by other disciplines. For instance, an early-American history course, "Whose Country is this Anyway? Rewriting America's History," focused on people of color, regroups a cohort of twenty-five advanced composition/reading ESL students in a class of fifty to 150 students.

Ongoing assessment and research based on data collection and analysis is viewed as a critical means for sustaining, improving, and expanding the LinC Program. With the support of the college and the district's institutional researchers, multiple assessment measures are used, including the Student Profile, success and persistence rates, Small Group Instructional Feedback (SGIF), reflective student essays, a student survey, and a faculty survey. Learning communities with consistently high retention and success rates include: LART reading and writing linked with counseling and tutorial components; LART reading and writing, a counseling component, and a general education/transfer Speech Communication class; ESL, a general education/transfer American History class with counseling and tutorial components; and, Developmental Math and Introduction to Sociology with counseling and tutorial components.

An important feature of De Anza's learning community work is the extensive, ongoing faculty development program undertaken in collaboration with the Office of Staff and Organizational Development. Expectations and guidelines for designing, implementing, and assessing learning community curriculum are explicit; faculty who want to teach in a learning community are supported by workshops and in-service professional development. For instance, all faculty, including adjuncts, are introduced to Classroom Assessment Techniques (CATs), a collection of informal feedback strategies developed by faculty across the country and collected by Thomas Angelo and K. Patricia Cross (1993). These CATs, from the simple "muddiest point" to the more complex "Paper or Project Prospectus," enable classroom teachers to find out how effective their teaching is based on what students are learning. Faculty are also introduced to the LinC Program's use of Small Group Instructional Feedback (SGIF) where staff routinely administer SGIF's in the fourth and tenth week of the quarter so students can collectively reflect on what is and is not working in their learning community. An analysis of student feedback is used to identify areas where faculty, collectively, need more training. The college provides budgetary support for conference travel, release time, stipends, workshops, and a retreat off campus every quarter for faculty and staff in the LinC Program and anyone else who is interested.

Website: http://www.deanza.fhda.edu/linc
Coordinator: Edwina Stoll, stolledwina@fhda.edu

Regional Learning Communities Consortium (RLCC): http://www.cal-rlcc.org Created in 1999, the consortium includes De Anza and eleven other community colleges from four counties in Northern California. In 2000, the consortium received funding to support the design of learning community curricula, introduce faculty to learning community pedagogy and assessment, and further collaboration among consortium members. The RLCC continues to build on its early work on improving teaching and learning for underrepresented and underprepared students.

Reference
Angelo, T. A., and K. P. Cross. 1993. *Classroom Assessment Techniques: A Handbook for College Teachers*. 2nd ed. San Francisco: Jossey-Bass.

Project Success: Grossmont Community College

We learn as much about ourselves as our academic studies.

—Project Success students

At Grossmont Community College in San Diego, California, Project Success teaches to the whole student. This philosophy continues to inform an award-winning program that has grown from a single experimental developmental reading and developmental writing link in 1985 to more than fifty links in 2003. Described as a program "for strengthening skills and promoting cooperative learning." Project Success began in developmental education and now provides fundamental and transfer program strands. Of 1,200 to 1,500 students annually involved in Project Success, 600 are developmental students.

In the fundamental strand, Project Success combines developmental reading and developmental writing at two levels, reading and writing (English 105 with English 101), and reading and composition (English 106 with English 110). English 105 and English 106 provide specific instruction in comprehension skills, vocabulary improvement, and college reading techniques; English 101 focuses on paragraph and essay development while English 110 emphasizes more sophisticated essay forms.

The program's continued attraction for developmental students—now promoted by word of mouth—is the selection of books that people read, talk, and write about each semester . . .

The program's continued attraction for developmental students—now promoted by word of mouth—is the selection of books that people read, talk, and write about each semester, such as *Warriors Don't Cry*, *The Color of Water*, and *It is not about the Bike*. Typically, the books are nonfiction and their authors are courageous people whose stories inspire others to do their best. In a learning environment where the majority of students' lives often reflect the "barriers" described in research on at-risk students, themes about overcoming challenges engage people in personal ways. In turn, the connections students draw between their experience and the course content provides anxious learners with a less threatening entry point for developing academic abilities.

The majority of Project Success students move from one developmental reading and developmental writing link to the next level or to transfer links that combine general education English courses with general education courses in other academic fields and disciplines such as humanities, psychology, history, and speech. Honors courses are now included in this learning communities program. Project Success faculty encourage all students to develop study groups that share common goals.

The story of Project Success speaks to the wisdom of building on what works for students and for faculty. In an institution where low class enrollments are not acceptable and no release time or stipends are available to integrate curriculum, Project Success invites faculty to work collaboratively in the context of a learning community model that most closely resembles their actual teaching assignments and working conditions. When the program began to expand in response to student demand, the two founding faculty looked for colleagues who they thought would enjoy working collaboratively. As Mary Donnelly and Sue Jensen report, "we simply sell it to our colleagues as the most rewarding teaching any of us has ever done. We enjoy teaching with another colleague and helping students see that knowledge and ideas transfer from one class to another. We just really believe in it and love it and a lot of our colleagues who teach these links agree with us." Since sections have been added slowly over the years, new teachers are partnered with veterans who serve as mentors. Faculty teams work hard to integrate curriculum and assignments, and meet regularly to track each student's personal and intellectual development and to discuss the program's philosophy and implications for teaching practice.

Two studies conducted by the Office of Research, Planning, and Academic Services document the program's success. A 1995 study confirmed earlier research done by Donnelly: students participating in learning communities had higher success, retention, persistence, and transition rates than comparable students in equivalent non-Project Success classes. A 2000 study compared program data from fall 1996 to spring 2000: Project Success students had higher retention, persistence, and transfer rates than their counterparts enrolled in the same two developmental levels of English courses; they also had a higher mean semester GPA. In fall 2001, a survey of 313 students included these responses: 72 percent took Project Success because they thought a combined course would help them improve their skills; 89 percent had not been enrolled in a Project Success link; and 88 percent would enroll in another Project Success learning community link.

Website: http://www.grossmont.net
Contact: Sue Jensen, sue.Jensen@gcccd.net

Tribal Environmental and Natural Resources Management (TENRM) Program: Northwest Indian College, Lummi Nation

A by-product of TENRM is the self-esteem, pride, and identity among students. They use terms like 'my people.' They know what it means to have a voice. They have their own ideas. They see people at eye-level rather than viewing themselves as inferior.

—Phil Duran, TENRM director.

The multidisciplinary core courses are taught in four- to five-hour blocks, four days a week, with a focus on "active connections within the natural world" rather than compartmentalized knowledge.

TENRM is a multidisciplinary environmental studies program at Northwest Indian College (NWIC) in Bellingham, Washington, one of thirty-three tribal colleges in the United States. The two-year program prepares Native American and Alaskan Native students for tribal natural resources management and environmental work by emphasizing practical competency—the ability to understand and solve complex real-world problems. Graduates work for their tribes as technical experts or transfer to four-year institutions to complete undergraduate degrees, often in environmental studies, and then do advanced work for their tribes.

TENRM was designed to meet the needs expressed by leaders from twenty-six Pacific Northwest tribes who called on educators to train future leaders who could address resource management issues within the context of community and culture. With funding from the National Science Foundation—and in partnership with Huxley College of the Environment and Fairhaven College at Western Washington University (WWU) and The Evergreen State College—NWIC began to develop TENRM's curriculum in 1997. The program's first students, representing ten tribes from Washington, Alaska, California, and New York, started their studies in fall 1998. Most of TENRM's students continue to be older, married with children.

The design and delivery of TENRM is based on a thematic and team-taught learning community model, an approach that most closely resembles Native American teaching and learning. Students and faculty enter the program as a cohort, the Native value of emphasizing the "interdependence of individuals across the community of learners" critical to the program's success (Berardi et al. 2002, 51). Students take sixty of the ninety credits required for an associate of arts and science degree with their cohort group and the remaining thirty credits as separate NWIC courses. Field trips, group projects, and internships are integral to the six-quarter program.

TENRM curriculum combines natural sciences, political science, public policy, and management with cultural experience and support. The multidisciplinary core courses are taught in four- to five-hour blocks, four days a week, with a focus on "active connections within the natural world" rather than compartmentalized knowledge. Phil Duran, TENRM's first director, describes how principles of learning communities and Indian values and learning styles inform the day-to-day activities of students and faculty.

The kind of learning we are trying to facilitate takes place in a circle. Our small circle of learning can merge with others springing up to form bigger ones. Because the schools have taught us to be linear thinkers, it may take a special effort to discover our other powers. The libraries and the Internet are full of resources we can search on our own at any time—and in TENRM you are required to use them—but the way of the circle is holistic, compassionate, spiritual, ecological, communal, experiential, practical, and *oral*. This kind of learning is active; it hones your critical thinking skills; it can only be experienced together. It works only if there is someone to listen when someone speaks, if there is someone who will speak when someone needs to hear it. This is an important part of the TENRM journey. (Berardi et al. 2001, 18)

Each quarter is organized with a unifying theme. For instance, "To Be the Eagle's View" introduces an Indian and Alaskan Native perspective for examining similarities and differences between tribal and western science. This first quarter, which helps students develop an understanding of the relationship of scientific concepts and basic environmental sciences terminology to tribal issues, also focuses on developing students' basic writing, reading, and computational skills. The next three quarters focus on the cultural and economic importance of water, land and land use, and oceans. The fifth quarter, "Making Connections, Finding a Balance," explores the complex connections among cultural values, economic development, and environmental protection faced by tribal resource managers and leaders responsible for sustaining community development in Indian nations. The final quarter, "Bringing It All Together," requires students to design, implement, analyze, and present a community-based, capstone group project on an environmental issue.

Since TENRM's founding, three fundamental principles have guided the program: co-articulation of tribal and western knowledge, a policy of non-abandonment, and an emphasis on developmental education. The first describes TENRM's efforts to align instruction in resource management with traditional values and knowledge, a curricular aim since TENRM's inception. The program is strengthened by the cultural teachings of visiting and resident Indian and Alaskan Native scholars and leaders who are often present in the classroom. The second principle, the non-abandonment policy, became an explicit practice as a consequence of faculty's struggle with students' attendance and varying performance levels. While standards are not lowered for students who have difficulty with their studies, no formal action is taken to remove students from the program if they fail to attend class or complete their course credits on schedule. The third principle, developmental education, expresses the determination of the original six TENRM faculty, two WWU professors of environmental physical and social sciences and four faculty from NWIC—a biologist, a chemist, a mathematician and computer specialist, and a Lummi Nation member/cultural specialist/anthropologist—to build on incoming students' knowledge and levels of preparation. While students work hard to develop basic academic abilities, their personal and practical experiences enrich the program's integrated curriculum from the first day of classes.

Student success is based on work completed inside and outside the classroom. Conventional testing in written and oral formats occurs on a regular basis, but community members and faculty also observe how students teach one another complex material, work with the community during tribal internships,

The program is strengthened by the cultural teachings of visiting and resident Indian and Alaskan Native scholars and leaders who are often present in the classroom.

Success includes whether a student stays grounded in cultural values, maintains self-respect and a healthy sense of self within the context of community, uses critical and integrative abilities to problem solve and imagine creative solutions, and makes substantial improvements in writing, reading comprehension, speaking, and mathematics.

and work with team members during their TENRM capstone project. Success includes whether a student stays grounded in cultural values, maintains self-respect and a healthy sense of self within the context of community, uses critical and integrative abilities to problem solve and imagine creative solutions, and makes substantial improvements in writing, reading comprehension, speaking, and mathematics.

In many Native American education programs, retention rates are low. As teaching team members note, students' personal circumstances such as "family responsibilities, legal and financial problems, chemical dependencies, domestic abuse, lack of self-confidence, and coming to terms with one's place in American society as a Native American" make staying in school very difficult (Berardi et al. 2002, 58). Of the nineteen students enrolled in the first TENRM cohort in fall 1998, ten were still enrolled in the last quarter of their two-year program (two students had died). Six received associate of arts in sciences degrees and transferred to universities; the other four stayed in TENRM until they completed their two-year degree. Student participation and retention continues to improve: after the first year, the second cohort's retention rate was 87 percent and the third cohort's retention rate was 100 percent (LaFrance 2003, iv).

Website: http://www.nwic.edu/tenrm
Contact: Northwest Indian College Telephone: 360-392-4309

References

Berardi, G., D. Burns, P. Duran, R. Gonzalez-Plaza, S. Kinley, L. Robbins, T. Williams, and W. Woods. 2001. *Handbook for Facilitators: Principles and Adaptation of the Tribal Environmental and Natural Resources Management (TENRM) Model for Tribal Colleges.* Bellingham, WA: Northwest Indian College.

Berardi, G., D. Burns, P. Duran, R. Gonzalez-Plaza, S. Kinley, L. Robbins, T. Williams, and W. Woods. 2002. "Science and Culture in a Curriculum for Tribal Environmental Management: The Tenrm Program at the Northwest Indian College." *American Indian Culture and Research Journal* 26(3): 45-62.

LaFrance, J. 2003. *TENRM Evaluation Report – 2001/2002 Academic Year.* Unpublished paper prepared for the National Science Foundation, TENRM Advisory Board, and Northwest Indian College. Bellingham, WA.

Circle of Learning for Entering Students: University of Texas at El Paso

The University of Texas at El Paso (UTEP) serves a large, binational, bicultural population located on the U.S.-Mexico border. The student population reflects the demographics of the region from which UTEP draws 90 percent of its more than 17,000 students: 69 percent Hispanic, 14 percent African American, 1.3 percent Asian, 0.3 percent Native American, and 13 percent international. UTEP ranks second in the nation in awarding bachelor's degrees to Hispanics and is in the top ten in bachelor's degrees awarded to Hispanics in business, engineering, and health sciences.

At UTEP, many students are first-generation and considered "at risk" in higher education. The Circle of Learning for Entering Students (CircLES) program was piloted in 1997 as a student support component of the Model Institutions for Excellence (MIE) initiative, funded by the National Science Foundation. UTEP was one of six institutions selected to develop new models in undergraduate education to increase minorities' involvement in the fields of science, technology, engineering, and mathematics. Designed for twenty-five entering science and engineering students, CircLES includes a mandatory weeklong summer orientation, personalized advising and mentoring, and a learning communities' cluster (a mathematics course, an English course, a Seminar in Critical Inquiry, and a discipline-specific course). After the first pilot of sixty students, the program was scaled up to include all first-time, full-time students.

The first CircLES pilot served pre-calculus students, but the program soon expanded to include developmental students. Before or on the first day of the summer orientation, students take math and English placement tests. During the week, students attend a six-hour math review taught by junior and senior students and then work in small groups of three to four students to brush up on math skills. At the end of the week, they take the math placement test again. Forty percent place in a higher level of math, pre-calculus or Calculus I, saving them one semester; these students consistently do as well as regularly admitted students.

In the fall of 2002, 409 of the 488 students from the summer orientation were placed in CircLES clusters. Students not placed either needed to take ESL classes or they could not attend school full time. Eighteen learning communities were offered: three calculus clusters, eight pre-calculus clusters, five intermediate algebra clusters, and two introductory algebra clusters—that is, among UTEP's pre-science and pre-engineering students, 38 percent are developmental mathematics students. In English, two of the four courses in the sequence are also developmental, noncredit courses.

Counselors and UTEP science and engineering graduates are integral to CircLES' success. They provide academic advising, career planning, and mentoring. UTEP also hires twenty-five undergraduate science and engineering majors to be peer mentors each year. Attached to CircLES' clusters through the Critical Inquiry seminar, a three-credit hour seminar taught by science and engineering professors and staff, the peer mentors participate in a weekly training and leadership program where they are introduced to cooperative teaching and learning strategies. Each seminar focuses on five UTEP freshmen learning goals including problem solving.

During the week, students attend a six-hour math review taught by junior and senior students and then work in small groups of three to four students to brush up on math skills.

Before implementing CircLES, the first-year retention rate for science, technology, engineering, and mathematics students was a little under 70 percent; since CircLES, the retention rate is a consistent 80 percent. Disaggregated data for developmental students indicates that they have gained most from the program.

Website: http://univstudies.utep.edu
Contact: Cathy Willermet, cwillermet@utep.edu

III

Additional Resources

Additional Resources

Learning Communities Websites

In addition to websites at individual institutions, there are three premier websites that have extensive information on learning communities and freshman seminars.

http://learningcommons.evergreen.edu is the website of the Washington Center's National Learning Communities Project, located at The Evergreen State College. This site includes a bibliography, a national directory of learning communities in the United States, an online forum, and various useful resources on getting started and sustaining learning communities and assessment.

www.sc.edu/fye is the site of the National Resource Center for The First-Year Experience and Students in Transition at the University of South Carolina. This website offers information on their conferences, publications, and research. Especially notable are their national surveys of first-year programming.

www.brevard.edu/fyc is the website of the Policy Center on the First Year of College, which includes information on assessment, research reports, and forums and institutes pertaining to the first year of college.

Developmental Education and Related Websites

www.nade.net is the site of the National Association for Developmental Education, which provides information on best practices, statistics, and professional standards (including NADE self-evaluation guides). It also offers program certification for tutoring services, developmental coursework, and adjunct instructional programs.

www.ncde.appstate.edu is the National Center for Developmental Education site, which provides a comprehensive archive of articles, research resources, and publications (including the *Journal of Developmental Education*).

www.ncde.appstate.edu/kellogg.htm is the Kellogg Institute site, which offers advanced training program for developmental educators and learning skills specialists. The Institute is located at the Appalachian State University in affiliation with the National Center for Developmental Education.

www.crla.net is the College Reading and Learning Association site, which provides links to related organizations, a calendar of events, and publication resources, including the *Journal of College Reading and Learning*. CRLA also offers certification for tutor and peer mentor programs.

www.eiu.edu/~lrnasst/nclca/index.html is the National College Learning Center Association site, which offers the *Learning Assistance Review* publication.

www.ntatutor.org is the National Tutoring Association site, which offers certification as a peer tutor, paraprofessional, professional tutor, or tutor trainer/administrator. Three levels of certification are available: Basic, Advanced, and Master.

www.rit.edu/~jwsldc/NYCLSA/index.shtml is the New York College Learning Skills Association site, which offers the *Journal of Research and Teaching in Developmental Education.*

www.umkc.edu/cad/si/ is the Center for Supplemental Instruction site, located at the University of Missouri-Kansas City, which offers workshop information and publication material in the areas supplemental education.

Written Publications

There is a large collection of literature on learning communities available at the National Learning Communities Project website referenced above. The following literature is a highly selective list that provides a good starting place for those interested in reading more about learning communities.

Learning Community Rationale and Practice

Cross, K. P. 1998. "Why Learning Communities? Why Now?" *About Campus.* 3(3), 1998: 4-11.

Gabelnick, F., J. MacGregor, R. Matthews, and B. L. Smith. 1990. *Learning Communities: Creating Connections Among Students, Faculty and Disciplines.* New Directions for Teaching and Learning, 41. San Francisco: Jossey-Bass.

Guarasci, R., and G. H. Cornwell. 1997. *Democratic Education in an Age of Difference.* San Francisco: Jossey-Bass.

Ratcliff and Associates. 1995. Realizing the Potential: Improving Postsecondary Teaching, Learning and Assessment. *University Park, PA: National Center on Postsecondary Teaching, Learning, and Assessment.*

Schoem, D. "Transforming Undergraduate Education, Moving Beyond Distinct Undergraduate Initiatives." *Change* 34(6), (2002): 51-55.

Shapiro, N., and J. Levine. 1999. *Creating Learning Communities: A Practical Guide to Winning Support, Organizing for Change, and Implementing Programs.* San Francisco: Jossey-Bass.

Smith, B. L., and J. McCann, eds. 2001. *Re-Inventing Ourselves: Interdisciplinary Education, Collaborative Learning, and Experimentation in Higher Education.* Bolton, MA: Anker Publishing.

Smith, B. L., J. MacGregor, R. Matthews, and F. Gabelnick. Forthcoming. *Learning Communities: Reforming Undergraduate Education. San Francisco: Jossey- Bass.*

Tagg, J. 2003. *The Learning Paradigm College.* Bolton, MA: Anker Publishing Company.

Tinto, V. 2002. *Learning Better Together: The Impact of Learning Communities on Student Success.* Higher Education Program, Syracuse University, Syracuse, New York. http://soeweb.syr.edu/faculty/Vtinto/index.html.

Tinto, V. "Taking Retention Seriously: Rethinking the First Year of College." *NACADA Journal.* 19(2), (2000): 5-10.

Tinto, V. 1993. *Leaving College: Rethinking the Causes and Cures of Student Attrition.* 2nd ed. Chicago: The University of Chicago Press.

Tinto, V. "Classrooms as Communities: Exploring the Educational Character of Student Persistence." *Journal of Higher Education.* 68(6), (1997): 599-623.

Pedagogy

Angelo, T. A., and K. P. Cross. 1993. *Classroom Assessment Techniques.* 2nd ed. San Francisco: Jossey-Bass.

Bean, J. 1996. *Engaging Ideas: The Professor's Guide to Integrating Writing, Critical Thinking, and Active Learning in the Classroom.* San Francisco: Jossey-Bass.

Cross, K. P., C. H. Major, and E. Barkley. Forthcoming. *Collaborative Learning Techniques: A Practical Guide to Promoting Learning in Groups.* San Francisco: Jossey Bass.

Finkel, D. 2001. *Teaching with Your Mouth Shut.* Portsmouth, NH: Heinemann.

MacGregor, J., ed. 1993. *Student Self-Evaluation: Fostering Reflective Learning.* New Directions in Teaching and Learning, 56. San Francisco: Jossey-Bass.

MacGregor, J., J. L. Cooper, K. A. Smith, and P. Robinson. 2000. *Strategies for Energizing Large Classes: From Small groups to Learning Communities.* New Directions in Teaching and Learning, 81. San Francisco: Jossey-Bass.

Millis, B., and P. Cottell, Jr. 1998. *Cooperative Learning for Higher Education Faculty.* American Council on Education Series on Higher Education. Phoenix: Oryx Press.

Schilling, K. M., and K. L. Schilling. "Increasing Expectations for Student Effort." *About Campus* 4(2) (1999): 4-10.

Spear, K. 1988. *Sharing Writing: Peer Response Groups in English Classes.* Portsmouth, NH: Boynton/Cook Publishers.

van Slyck, P. "Repositioning Ourselves in the Contact Zone." *College English,* 59(2): (1997): 149-170.

Learning Communities Implementation and Assessment

Elliott, J., and E. Decker. 1999. "Garnering the Fundamental Resources for Learning Communities." J. H. Levine, ed. *Learning Communities: New Structures, New Partnerships for Learning.* Columbia, SC: University of South Carolina, National Resource Center for the First-Year Experience and Students in Transition.

Geri, L., D. Kuehn, and J. MacGregor. 1999. "From Innovation to Reform: Reflections on Case Studies of 19 Learning Community Initiatives." In *Strengthening Learning Communities: Case Studies from the National Learning Communities Dissemination Project (FIPSE),* compiled by J. MacGregor. Olympia, WA: The Evergreen State College, Washington Center for Improving the Quality of Undergraduate Education, 195-203.

Koolsbergen, W. "Approaching Diversity: Some Classroom Strategies for Learning Communities." *Peer Review,* Summer/Fall (2001).

Laufgraben, J. L., and N. Shapiro, eds. Forthcoming. *Learning Communities in Context: A Practical Guide to Sustaining Change, Expanding Support, and Improving Programs.* San Francisco: Jossey-Bass.

MacGregor, J., and others. 2003a. *Integrating Learning Communities with Service-Learning.* National Learning Communities Project Monograph Series. Olympia, WA: The Evergreen State College, Washington Center for Improving the Quality of Undergraduate Education, in cooperation with the Association for Higher Education.

MacGregor, J., and others. 2003b. *Doing Learning Community Assessment: Five Campus Stories.* National Learning Communities Project Monograph Series. Olympia, WA: The Evergreen State College, Washington Center for Improving the Quality of Undergraduate Education in cooperation with the American Association for Higher Education.

MacGregor, J., V. Tinto, and J. H. Lindblad. 2000. "Assessment of Innovative Efforts: Lessons from the Learning Community Movement." In *Assessment to Promote Deep Learning: Insights from AAHE's 2000 and 1999 Assessment Conferences.* L. Suskie, ed. Washington, DC: American Association for Higher Education, 1-6.

Developmental Education

Boylan, H. R. 2002. *What Works: Research-Based Best Practices in Developmental Education.* Boone, NC: Continuous Quality Improvement Network with the National Center for Developmental Education.

Higbee, J. L., and Dwinell, P. 1998. *Developmental Education; Preparing Success for College Students.* Columbia, SC: National Center for the First-Year Experience and Students in Transition, University of South Carolina.

Lundell, D. B, and J. L. Higbee, eds. 2001. *Theoretical Perspectives for Developmental Education.* Minneapolis, MN: Center for Research on Developmental Education and Urban Literacy, University of Minnesota, General College.

Lundell, D. B, and J. L. Higbee, eds. 2002 *History of Developmental Education.* Minneapolis, MN: Center for Research on Developmental Education and Urban Literacy, University of Minnesota, General College.

McCabe, R. H. 2000. *No One to Waste: A Report to Public Decision-Makers and Community College Leaders.* Washington, DC: Community College Press.

McCabe, R. H. 2003. *Yes We Can! A Community College Guide for Developing America's Underprepared.* League for Innovation in the Community College and American Association of Community Colleges.

McCabe, R. H., and P. R. Day Jr., eds. 1998. *Developmental Education: A Twenty-First Century Social and Economic Imperative.* Mission Viejo, CA: League for Innovation in the Community College and The College Board.

Roueche, J. E., and S. Roueche. 1993. *Between a Rock and a Hard Place: The At-Risk Student in the Open Door College.* Washington, DC: Community College Press.

Roueche, J. E., and S. Roueche. 1999. *High Stakes, High Performance: Making Remedial Education Work.* Washington, DC: American Association of Community Colleges.

Contributors

Pam Dusenberry teaches in the Developmental English Program at Shoreline Community College where for the last fourteen years she has been working to integrate the Developmental English curriculum of reading, writing and study skills, and to bring to it what is known about human learning from psychology, linguistics, neurobiology, and educational research. Dusenberry has also been involved in developing abilities-based assessment of student learning where students move through the curriculum based on their performance as readers and writers; a portfolio process allows students to "jump" classes based on their work. SCC also offers Integrated Studies courses that include a developmental component where Dusenberry also has taught. She is co-author with Dutch Henry and T. Sean Rody of *College Knowledge*, a collection of challenging readings for students new to academic culture; the book also includes an account of the instructional practices used in Shoreline's integrated Developmental English Program. Dusenberry has presented her work at the National Learning Communities Project Summer Institutes and has given workshops at conferences and retreats on learning communities and developmental education. Pam can be reached at PamDuse@aol.com.

Gillies Malnarich co-directs the Washington Center for Improving the Quality of Undergraduate Education at The Evergreen State College. She was first introduced to interdisciplinary studies as a student in the inaugural class of Arts One at the University of British Columbia, a program shaped by the legacy of Joseph Tussman. Educated in the humanities and social sciences, she has taught in and out of higher education: in workplaces, women's centers, community-based schools, and other adult education programs; and, at universities, a four-year college, and a large urban community college, Douglas College in New Westminster. There, she taught in Developmental Studies and created an in-house education program for faculty, staff, and administrators. She has worked with educators in Canada on abilities-based teaching, learning, assessment, and institutional effectiveness. At the Washington Center, she works with co-director Emily Lardner to support campuses experienced and new to learning communities by focusing on the design of integrated curricula and assignments, equity issues and preparing students for demanding college-level work, campus-based leadership, and ways to sustain and strengthen efforts. Malnarich can be reached at malnarig@evergreen.edu.

Ben Sloan, an Associate Professor of English, teaches developmental and college transfer courses at Piedmont Virginia Community College in Charlottesville, Virginia. As a developmental writing instructor, Sloan helped prepare students to pass the CUNY Writing Assessment Test in his work as part of the SEEK program at John Jay College in New York City (1983-89). He taught developmental writing and other English courses in women's and men's prisons while working for Shaw University in Raleigh NC (1991-95). At Fayetteville Technical Community College (FTCC), Sloan taught developmental reading and writing as well as college transfer classes for eight years (1995-2003), during which time he worked with an interdisciplinary team, associated with a College Tech Prep project, to develop professional development activities for faculty and staff, including a career awareness program for at-risk eighth graders. In 2000, he attended the Kellogg Institute at Appalachian State University. Between 2001 and 2003 he helped design and then taught in a learning community project at FTCC. He is the Excellence in Teaching Award winner at FTCC for 2002-03. Sloan can be reached at bsloan@pvcc.edu.

Jan Swinton is an English instructor and the Faculty Development Coordinator at Spokane Falls Community College in Spokane, Washington. She is the past director of the College's Developmental Reading, Writing, and Study Skills Program. She has taught composition, developmental reading/developmental writing, and college-level study skills classes as well as reading and study skills courses paired with content classes such as biology, gerontology, and elementary algebra. She is the co-author with W. J. Agopsowicz of *Read and Respond*, a developmental reading textbook in its fourth edition. She chairs the "Paired Courses" Special Interest Group for the College Reading and Learning Association (CRLA) and has served as president of the regional organizations of CRLA and the National Association of Developmental Education. Recently re-elected as president of the Washington Association of Developmental Education, she works with developmental educators throughout the State. Swinton presents at regional and national conferences and is a fellow with the National Learning Communities Project. Swinton can be reached at JanS@spokanefalls.edu.

Phyllis van Slyck is a professor in the English Department at LaGuardia. With her colleague William J. Koolsbergen of the Humanities Department, she has been instrumental in the design and expansion of various learning community models at the college for the last decade. She coordinates faculty development activities related to learning communities, serves as liaison between faculty and administration to evaluate newly proposed learning communities, and hosts visits from other colleges interested in developing learning communities. With Professor Koolsbergen, she has given numerous workshops at colleges and universities, and with other learning community colleagues, at national conferences. LaGuardia Community College has been involved in the design and development of learning communities since 1976 and is a member of the newly formed Atlantic Center for Learning Communities, a regional branch of the learning community movement that offers resource consulting, open houses that showcase learning communities' practice, on-campus site visits, and retreats for faculty/administration/campus teams interested in deepening their understanding of learning communities, related pedagogies and assessment. She is a fellow with the National Learning Communities Project. van Slyck can be reached at vanph@lagcc.cuny.edu.

25

National Learning Communities Project
Monograph Series

Integrating Learning Communities with Service-Learning
  Jean MacGregor with Marie Eaton, Richard Guarasci, Maria Hesse,
  Gary Hodge, Ted Lewis, Marybeth Mason, Judith Patton, Lin Nelson, John
  O'Connor, Penny Pasque, and David Schoem.

Learning Communities and Diversity
  Emily Decker Lardner with others.

*Learning Communities and Fiscal Reality: Optimizing Learning in a Time
  of Restricted Resources*
  Al Guskin, Mary Marcy, and Barbara Leigh Smith

Learning Communities in Community Colleges
  Julia Fogarty and Lynn Dunlap, with Edmund Dolan, Maria Hesse,
  Marybeth Mason, and Jacque Mott.

Learning Communities in Liberal Arts Colleges
  Karen Spear, with J. David Arnold, Grant H. Cornwell, Eve Walsh Stoddard,
  Richard Guarasci, and Roberta S. Matthews.

Learning Communities in Research Universities
  John O'Connor, with James A. Anderson, Jodi Levine Laufgraben,
  Karen Oates, David Schoem, Nancy S. Shapiro, and Barbara Leigh Smith.

*The Pedagogy of Possibilities: Developmental Education, College-Level
  Studies, and Learning Communities*
  Gillies Malnarich with others.

What We Know Now about Learning Community Research and Assessment
  Kathe Taylor, with William Moore, Jean MacGregor, and Jerri Lindblad.

Doing Learning Community Assessment: Five Campus Stories
  Jean MacGregor, with Michelle D. Cook, Lynn Dunlap, Shari Ellerston,
  Doug Epperson, Teresa L. Flateby, Mary E. Huba, Phil Jenks, Yves
  Labissiere, Jodi Levine Laufgraben, William S. Moore, Judy Patton, and
  Les Stanwood.

Learning Communities and the Academic Library
  Sarah Pedersen.